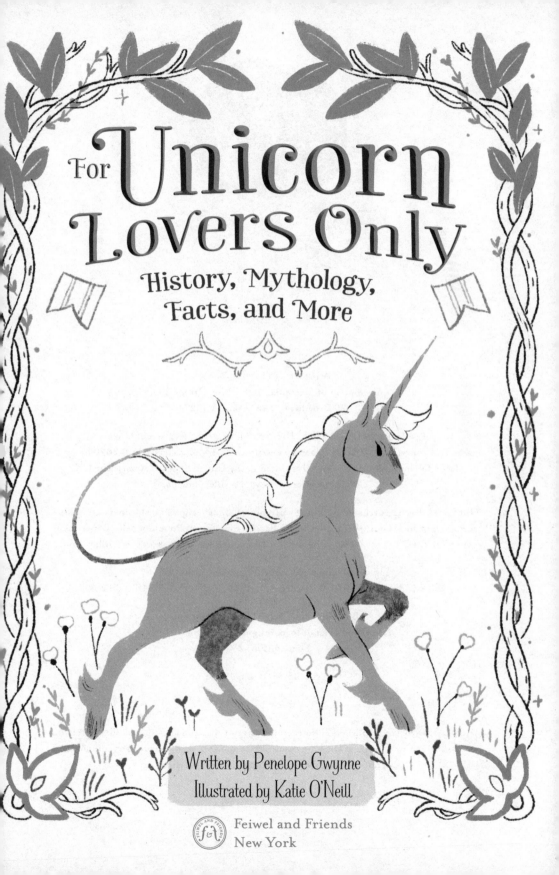

For Unicorn Lovers Only

History, Mythology, Facts, and More

Written by Penelope Gwynne

Illustrated by Katie O'Neill

Feiwel and Friends
New York

A Feiwel and Friends Book
An imprint of Macmillan Publishing Group, LLC
120 Broadway, New York, NY 10271

For Unicorn Lovers Only: History, Mythology, Facts, and More.
Text copyright © 2020 by Penelope Gwynne. Illustrations copyright © 2020 by
Katie O'Neill. All rights reserved. Printed in the United States of America by LSC
Communications, Crawfordsville, Indiana.

Our books may be purchased in bulk for promotional, educational, or business use. Please
contact your local bookseller or the Macmillan Corporate and Premium Sales Department
at (800) 221-7945 ext. 5442 or by email at MacmillanSpecialMarkets@macmillan.com.

Library of Congress Control Number: 2020908667
ISBN 978-1-250-75939-9 (hardcover) / ISBN 978-1-250-75940-5 (ebook)

Book design by Sarah Nichole Kaufman
Feiwel and Friends logo designed by Filomena Tuosto
First edition, 2020

1 3 5 7 9 10 8 6 4 2

mackids.com

For Freddie, Space Commander —P.G.

For Alex —K.O.

TABLE OF CONTENTS

So you love unicorns . . .

Why wouldn't you? With their rainbow manes and glittery hooves, unicorn magic and adorable friendship dramas, unicorns are some of the friendliest mythical creatures. They prance through cartoons and picture books and make some of the *most* adorable stuffed animals.

Or is that not the kind of unicorn you were thinking of?

Maybe you had something a little more majestic in mind: an elegant equine galloping through a meadow, its pristine white coat shimmering in the sunlight, long mane and tail streaming behind. What could be more romantic than the unicorn of legend—a wild, magical creature that cannot be tamed?

Truth be told, they're both pretty hard to resist. But which one is the *real* unicorn?

They both are. Each is the unicorn of its time and place, variations on a creature that may have changed more than any other over the past two thousand years. Centuries ago, unicorns were pocket-sized pets—little lap goats with beards and cloven hooves that perched on ladies' laps in paintings. Before that, they were murderous, feral animals whose eyes glowed red. Like any good mythical beast, unicorns reflect the hopes and fears of their storytellers. Sometimes they also boogie down and shovel snow.

Whichever kind of unicorn you prefer, there's a world full of adventures and lore out there just waiting for you to go looking for it.

You can make your own unicorn magic, whether it's real or imagined, if you're willing to go for it. I hope this book will start you on your way.

Your unicorn guide,

Penelope Gwynne

History of Unicorns

How long have there been unicorns? Possibly as long as there have been humans to tell stories about them.

In Dordogne, France, some of the world's oldest cave paintings are preserved at Lascaux. Giant animals, painted about 17,000 years ago in bold lines of black, brown, and red, sprawl across the ceilings and walls of a system of underground caverns. Among the oxen, stags, deer, horses, and big cats, there is one mysterious creature archaeologists nicknamed the "unicorn," because of the long, straight horn that juts from its forehead.

Many people insist that Lascaux's unicorn actually has two horns, but unicorn lovers are free to draw their own conclusions about what the ancient painters intended. Even so, few people would recognize the creature in the caves as a relative of the animals we see in art today. Lumpy and spotted, with a short tail and a blunt nose, the Lascaux unicorn is a far cry from the graceful white horses that unicorns would later become.

Lascaux

When most people think of unicorns, they imagine a creature from a much later time: the Middle Ages. With flowing manes and spiral horns, they belong to the world of knights in armor and maidens in flowing gowns. And they come from a very specific place, too. The shining white horse-like unicorn that we know and love was first described in Europe. But unicorns throughout history and around the world have taken on many different forms.

And, truth be told, a lot of them looked more like the strange creature at Lascaux than the beautiful equines in our imaginations.

The history of the unicorn in Europe began around the fourth century BCE, in Greece. At the height of ancient Greek civilization, many scholars were interested in understanding and describing the natural world. Almost two thousand years before the printing press would be invented, they collected stories that described cultures and wildlife from other parts of the world in handwritten scrolls that could be copied by scribes and shared with other scholars.

Since it would also be thousands of years before cars, trains, or airplanes were invented, few scholars actually *saw* the creatures they were describing. Instead, they collected stories from travelers who spread out from Greece, mostly to trade with other cultures. This kind of information gathering allowed the ancient Greek philosophers to gain knowledge on subjects far beyond what they could have gathered on their own. But it also left room for a *lot* of mistakes. Stories were passed from one traveler to another, and like anyone playing a long game of telephone, scholars were likely to misinterpret at least some of the information.

One of those Greek scholars was a physician named Ctesias, who wrote about Persia and India. Ctesias was appointed as physician to the court of a Persian king (in what is now Iran), and lived there for seventeen years learning about Persian history and culture. When he returned to Greece in the year 398 BCE, he began writing two enormous scholarly works. One of them, called *Indica*, described what he had learned about India. (Although he called it India, Ctesias was probably referring to the region around Tibet.) While Ctesias had never made it to the land he was describing, he met travelers who had. Based on their stories, Ctesias wrote what was probably the first European story of a unicorn.

Ctesias's unicorn shared some qualities with the unicorn of today:

Ctesias

It was about the size of a horse and had a straight horn, about one and a half feet long, jutting from the middle of its forehead. But Ctesias's unicorn was a wild donkey, and while its body was white, its head was deep red and its eyes dark blue. Weirder still, its horn was three different colors: white at the base, black in the middle, and vivid red at the tip. It was an impressive beast. Ctesias said that the unicorn was "exceedingly swift and powerful" and no other animal could catch it. Strange though Ctesias's creature might seem to us today, it was the first many Europeans heard of the unicorn, and many, many later tales would be based on his description.

For more than 400 years, philosophers and scholars who mentioned unicorns mostly used Ctesias's description. The Roman naturalist Pliny the Elder included a unicorn in his *Naturalis Historia (Natural History)*. Pliny was still working on *Naturalis Historia* when he died during the eruption of Mount Vesuvius in 79 CE, but he had already created thirty-seven books in which he described animals from around the world. His unicorn was an "exceedingly wild beast called the Monoceros." According to Pliny, it had a stag's head, a horse's body, an elephant's feet, and a boar's tail. Its horn was solid black and more than two feet long. Like Ctesias's unicorn, it was also a fierce beast, and could not be captured alive.

Pliny

For centuries, the animal remained pretty much the same: A strange mash-up of stag, horse, and elephant continued to be described in texts. But with each new account, the unicorn gained more detail—and it became wilder. The length of the unicorn's horn grew over the years, and its temperament became more ferocious.

In the third century CE, a Roman named Aelian agreed with Pliny's description of the stag-headed, elephant-footed horse, but gave his unicorn the tail of a goat. He also added two important details: a mane and tawny coat. Aelian's unicorn was a solitary creature. Known to be gentle with other species, it would fiercely attack any other unicorns that came near it. Its horn, too, was deadly. It was almost three feet long, solid black, "not smooth, but covered in certain natural rings," and came to a wicked point.

Aelian

A century later, another Roman scholar named Julius Solinus described the unicorn as the "cruelest" monster. Although it looked much the same as the creature Aelian and Pliny described (except that it had the tail of a pig, rather than a boar or a goat), its behavior was far more ferocious than either of the earlier writers had believed. It "bellowed horribly," and its horn, now four feet long, was brightly colored and so sharp that it would instantly pierce anything the unicorn stabbed. It could be killed but was far too ferocious to ever be captured.

With its oversized horn, mix-and-match body, and cantankerous

Solinus

nature, it's not so surprising that the unicorn of the ancient Greeks and Romans didn't really catch on. The idea of the unicorn as a brightly colored Frankenstein's monster faded over time. But those early descriptions played a big part in shaping ideas about the unicorn's fierce and solitary nature, and also passed on an indispensable piece of information about unicorns: the magical properties of their horns. All the Greek and Roman scholars believed that drinking from a cup made of unicorn horn would heal epilepsy and neutralize poisons. That belief would last for thousands of years.

Over the years, unicorn horns were associated with all kinds of healing powers. See page 18 to learn more about alicorns!

In the end, the unicorn that endured was far cuter than Ctesias and Pliny had imagined. Diminutive goat-like creatures with snowy coats and graceful, spiraling horns, some were small enough to climb into a child's lap. It's not clear when these more friendly unicorns first appeared. But they probably owed some of their attributes to Julius Caesar.

Caesar

In the first century BCE, the Roman ruler wrote a series of reports describing his exploits in Gaul, an area that included much of modern-day Europe. In the sixth report, he listed some of the animals that could be found in the mysterious Hercynian Forest, a vast, dense wilderness that ran across what is now southern Germany. Along with the other creatures, Caesar described a stag that had a single long, straight horn on its forehead between its ears.

A similar creature made it into the bestiaries—collections of moral stories featuring animals—that began to pop up all around Europe two hundred years later. The first bestiary was probably created in Alexandria, Egypt. Copies of that original, called the *Physiologus*, would be created throughout Europe for centuries.

Unlike the stories of the ancient Greeks and Romans, who were trying to provide naturalistic accounts of animals found in the east, the bestiaries were designed to teach moral values. The books were much more popular than the writings of Ctesias and Pliny, and began to spread far and wide.

It would be more than a thousand years before the printing press was invented, so every copy of the bestiary was written out by hand. As each copy was made, the scribes who created it made changes, large and small, to the stories—many new bestiaries meant many new versions of the animal tales they told.

But all the bestiaries shared the same basic story about the unicorn: They described it as the size of a kid, or baby goat, with cloven (two-toed) hooves. Like earlier unicorns, this version was exceedingly fierce and couldn't be captured by men. But the bestiaries gave the key to trapping the wild beast: Hunters would leave a maiden alone in the woods where the unicorn was known to live. When it came across her, it would be so smitten that it would lay its head in her lap and allow itself to be captured.

Lascaux

Ctesias

Pliny

Aelian

UNICORN TIMELINE

Solinus

Caesar

As time went on, the unicorn became part of the culture and soon began to appear widely in art, often as a Christian religious symbol. By the Middle Ages, unicorns were often used as ornamentation (called illuminations) on religious manuscripts and in Bibles. They were carved into furniture, woven into tapestries, and worked into stained-glass windows.

The animals themselves continued to look quite different, depending on the artist who created them. Probably the best-known works of unicorn art from the Middle Ages is a series of tapestries known as the Unicorn Tapestries, woven in the Netherlands beginning in 1495. They show a white unicorn with a goatlike beard, cloven hooves, and a spiraling horn. But in a bestiary from the fourteenth century, the unicorn looks incredibly catlike. A tapestry woven in Switzerland around 1420 shows a spotted animal with the body of a horse, cloven hooves in the front, lion's paws in the back, and feathers around its neck. Another, created in Strasbourg, Germany, around 1500, shows a unicorn that looks a lot like a deer fawn, with long, spindly legs and a speckled brown coat.

Around the same time the Unicorn Tapestries were created, a boom in exploration began. Seeking new trade routes to Asia, European adventurers set out by ship to Africa, Central America, and North America. As they traveled through new lands, the explorers encountered plants and animals they had never seen before. Some were similar to the animals they had at home, but others were entirely different from European animals. They looked so outlandish, and behaved so oddly in the explorers' eyes, that they seemed a bit like mythical beasts. It wasn't such a stretch, then, when explorers began looking for unicorns wherever they went.

(After all, if you put a unicorn next to a giraffe or an ostrich, it doesn't seem so unusual.) During the sixteenth, seventeenth, and eighteenth centuries, reports of unicorns came in from all over the world.

The New World was supposedly full of them. In 1539, Friar Marcus of Nizza reported that he had seen the hide of a unicorn during a journey near Mexico. It was "half as big again as an ox," he said, and "had but one horn on his forehead, bending toward the breast."

Thirty years later, Sir John Hawkins reported that the indigenous people of Florida wore beads of unicorn horn around their necks. In 1673, Dr. Olfert Dapper reported seeing unicorns on the Canadian border, insisting that they had cloven hooves; rough manes; long, straight horns; black eyes; and necks like a stag's.

The possibility that unicorns might be found in Africa captured the imaginations of naturalists. Stories of one-horned antelopes, amphibians with cloven hooves in the front and webbed feet in the back, horned pachyderms, and, of course, one-horned equines continued to be told by travelers for hundreds of years.

In the 1620s, a missionary named Jerónimo Lobo returned from Abyssinia (what is now northern Ethiopia) with reports of having seen a unicorn that was the exact size and shape of a beautiful horse. It looked much like the unicorns we see in movies and artwork today, but was bay-colored and had a black mane and tail.

In 1800, Sir John Barrow returned to England from South Africa with a story about finding a cave painting that depicted a unicorn. He was just one of the many travelers to Africa who insisted they had heard stories of unicorns from indigenous people there, or had even seen a one-horned animal themselves. The fourth edition of the *Encyclopedia Britannica* insisted, "There can, we think, be little doubt that the unicorn exists in Africa, not far north of the Cape of Good Hope, and perhaps, at some distant period it may be as well-known as the elephant or the hippopotamus is at present."

Unicorns were everywhere. No one could agree on what they looked like, but they were clearly here to stay.

WHERE IN THE WORLD WERE THE UNICORNS?

For centuries, travelers from all over the world returned to Europe with stories of unicorns. Many were retelling stories that they had heard on their journeys. A few insisted they had seen the animals themselves. Put all these reports together, and they form a picture of a world in which unicorns could be anywhere. Here are just some of the places where unicorns were reported to live.

UNICORN SIGHTING

Tibet

Mount Sinai

Bhutan

Dar-Bagou

Mecca

India

Abyssinia

Strait of Malacca

Mountains of the Moon

Cape of Good Hope

How to Speak Unicorn

DUTCH—
eenhoorn

NORWEGIAN —
enhjørning

FRENCH—
licorne

PORTUGESE—
unicórnio

GERMAN—
Einhorn

RUSSIAN—
yedinorog

GREEK—
monókeros

SPANISH—
unicornio

ITALIAN—
unicorno

SWEDISH—
enhörning

A UNICORN BY ANY OTHER NAME

Unicorns may have appeared all over the world, but they certainly weren't the same in every place. Cultures around the world had their own versions of the magical, one-horned creatures. These magical animals may not have looked—or behaved—the same, but they all created a sense of awe and reverence in the cultures that created them. Here are a few.

CAMAHUETO

The Chiloé Archipelago, a series of islands that speckle the coast off the southern tip of South America, is home to a particularly destructive unicorn that spends much of its life in the sea. The camahueto is a giant bull with a single horn on its head. It is born in the mountains, where it springs from a piece of horn that has been planted in the dirt. Once it emerges, it makes directly for the ocean, destroying anyone in its path but creating new streams and rivers as it goes. It is up to a machi, or healer, to stop the bull and cut off its precious horn before it reaches the water.

KARKADANN

The Karkadann comes from India and Persia, and bears more than a passing

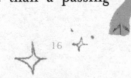

resemblance to Ctesias's Persian unicorn. Like that European creation, it is unfriendly to other Karkadann, can only be captured by a maiden, and its horn has magical, medicinal properties. But the Karkadann is built like a buffalo, has scaly black skin, and three yellow toes on each foot. In fact, the Karkadann looks an awful lot like a rhinoceros but has gained its own unique traits over the years.

QILIN

A far gentler unicorn appeared in Chinese stories as long ago as 2700 BCE. The qilin (pronounced chee-lin) is an extremely wise and peaceful beast. Much like some of the early European unicorns, it has the body of a stag, the tail of an ox, and the hooves of a horse, but that's about where the similarities end. The qilin is covered from head to hoof in multicolored scales, and some stories give it a wolflike head.

The qilin is considered the king of the beasts, but it does not rule by force. Unlike the ferocious unicorn, the qilin is so gentle that it will not eat living things—neither animals nor plants. It walks soundlessly, stepping carefully so that it will not even bend a blade of grass. And although it does have a large horn on its forehead, the horn is covered with flesh, making it unusable as a weapon.

The qilin is a good omen, a heavenly creature that comes to earth to bless the arrival of exceptionally good and wise rulers (one is also said to have appeared before the birth of the sage Confucius in the sixth century BCE). The qilin is also known to purify water by dipping in its horn.

ALL ABOUT ALICORNS

People all around Europe may have had different ideas about what unicorns looked like, but there was one fact they could agree on: Unicorn horns had medicinal—perhaps even magical—powers.

A unicorn's horn is called an alicorn. If you're up to date on your unicorns today, you probably know that sometimes winged unicorns are also called alicorns. How is that possible? Sometimes unicorns are just complicated like that. People have been calling the horns alicorns for nearly a thousand years. But in the 1980s, they started using the same name for winged unicorns.

In medieval Europe, alicorns (the horns) were more precious than gold. At one point, powdered "alicorn" was worth *ten times* its weight in gold. A whole horn was worth twice that. Powerful people—usually royalty or high-level church members—were willing to pay top dollar for even tiny specks of the stuff.

What made unicorn horn so desirable? It was believed to be a cure for all kinds of ailments. It was prescribed as a cure for epilepsy, the plague, and leprosy, as well as a host of other diseases. In a time before antibiotics, the supposed curative powers of powdered unicorn horn generated a lot of demand. But it was really the horn's ability to cure and prevent poisoning that drew the kings, queens, and popes of medieval Europe to it.

When Ctesias first described the unicorn back in the fourth century BCE, he mentioned the amazing powers of their horns. Drinking wine or water from a cup made of unicorn horn was said to cure poisoning—it would also prevent the person from being poisoned after they had drunk from the cup.

That was an appealing idea for the nobility of Europe, who were constantly worried that they might be poisoned by jealous family members scheming to take their thrones. Many kept unicorn horns as poison detectors in their dining rooms. They believed that if poison came near the horn, it would start to sweat, developing beads of moisture on its surface. As a result, unicorn horns were prized table decorations.

At the English wedding of Princess Margaret in the 1460s, an alicorn was placed in every corner of the banquet hall. In the French royal court, an alicorn was waved over the king's food in an elaborate ceremony before every meal. Powdered unicorn horn added to food was also said to neutralize poison, as was drinking from an alicorn cup.

Alicorns, often covered in gold and jewels, became a regular part of royal treasuries. They could also be found on display in government buildings and cathedrals. Probably the most famous alicorn belonged to the monastery of Saint-Denis in France. The seven-foot-long horn was kept with one end in a pool of water, from which visitors could drink. According to one traveler, people who drank from the water would immediately break out in a sweat.

Given the value of alicorn horns, people were willing to go to great lengths to find some to sell. People made "alicorn powder" out of everything from clay and limestone to dog bones and fossils. For that reason, powdered alicorn was rarely bought by the very rich. They preferred whole horns so they could be certain that the alicorn was real.

The enormous, spiraling horns that were so popular with the royals were most likely narwhal tusks. That doesn't necessarily mean that the sellers were trying to cheat their buyers—even narwhal tusks are rare, and anyone finding one might think they had stumbled across a genuine alicorn.

However, unscrupulous merchants faked whole horns, too. Walrus and elephant ivory could be chemically treated and straightened until it looked like alicorn. To avoid fakes, prospective buyers came up with elaborate tests that were believed to determine whether an alicorn was real. How any of the horns passed these magical tests is a mystery.

By the end of the seventeenth century, alicorns had fallen out of fashion with most royalty, but they remained a powerful symbol of healing. Unicorns often appeared on signs for apothecary shops. Medicines made from powdered horn, or made using water that had run through an alicorn, could still be found there. And alicorns, far more affordable now that they were no longer trendy, continued to be bought and sold.

Even with people who didn't believe in the medicinal powers of the horn, alicorns were in demand. In the seventeenth and eighteenth centuries, anyone who was anyone had a cabinet of curiosities. Sometimes it was just a cupboard; sometimes it was an entire room. Whatever it was, the cabinet was a place to display strange objects, both natural and magical, to show off to your friends. One of the most popular items for a well-stocked cabinet was unicorn horn.

How to Tell If Your Alicorn Is Real

Here are some simple—and not-so-simple—methods that medieval shoppers came up with to test the authenticity of an alicorn.

◊ **PLACE IT IN WATER.** A real alicorn will cause the water to bubble as if it is boiling, but the water will remain cold.

◊ **PUT IT IN** a container with some scorpions and place a heavy lid on top. After four hours, the scorpions should be dead.

◊ **PLACE THE HORN** near poison to see if it sweats.

◊ **DRAW A CIRCLE** with the horn (or with water in which the horn has been soaked) and place a spider inside it. If the alicorn is real, the spider will not be able to leave the circle.

◊ **POISON A PIGEON** with arsenic, then feed it powder from the horn. If the horn is real, the pigeon will be saved.

◊ **BURN IT.** Real alicorn gives off a sweet smell when burned. (But the bad news is that you just burned your very valuable unicorn horn.)

THE LION AND THE UNICORN

Over the centuries, unicorns had come to represent strength and fierceness—as well as religious virtue—so they were popular in coats of arms that represented noble households, and even entire countries. The unicorn became a symbol of Scotland in the twelfth century, when King William I added it to the royal coat of arms. In 1484, King James III of Scotland created currency that featured a unicorn. The gold coins were used for more than forty years before they were replaced.

For centuries, Scotland and England clashed in a series of wars.

They were finally united in 1603, when King James VI of Scotland took over the British monarchy. As a show of unity, a unicorn was added to the coat of arms for Great Britain, alongside the symbol of Britain, the lion.

Around that time, the nursery rhyme "The Lion and the Unicorn" became popular, probably inspired by the new coat of arms. It commemorated the long conflict between the two countries and their eventual union.

Today, the coat of arms of the United Kingdom is still supported by a lion and a unicorn, and the two beasts have appeared on the British pound coin, on government buildings and other architecture, on official communications and flags—wherever the coat of arms might be used. As it was on the Scottish arms, the unicorn is always chained, demonstrating the power of the monarchy—after all, it's a rare person who can tame the fierce unicorn.

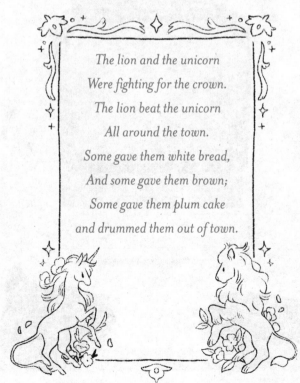

The lion and the unicorn
Were fighting for the crown.
The lion beat the unicorn
All around the town.
Some gave them white bread,
And some gave them brown;
Some gave them plum cake
and drummed them out of town.

PopCorn: Unicorns in Pop Culture

The twentieth century saw unicorns become the stars of fantasy novels and picture books, and as special effects became more realistic, they began to appear in movies, too. By the time the twenty-first century rolled around, unicorns were an entirely different creature. Today, you can find them tap-dancing and pooping rainbows. They're on your pajamas (your pillow might *be* a unicorn!) and lining the shelves of toy stores. You can even find unicorns on the stock market.

After two thousand years of mythology, unicorns have made the leap from legend to pop culture.

UNICORNS IN FICTION

Fiction writers have brought the unicorn legend forward by leaps and bounds in the last century. So if you're looking to spend time with some unicorns, head for the bookshelf. Of course, not all books about unicorns are created equal. Some feature sassy unicorn main characters. In others, unicorns appear more on the sidelines. Here are ten great books for getting your unicorn fix, in order (roughly) of most- to least-unicorny.

1. *The Last Unicorn* (1968)

Unicorns may appear in a lot of books, and may even have some pretty big roles, but they rarely get to take center stage. Perhaps that's why *The Last Unicorn* by Peter Beagle has become a classic. First published in 1968, the book has sold six million copies and is a favorite of unicorn lovers worldwide.

The story follows the adventures of a solitary unicorn who overhears a band of hunters saying that she must be the last unicorn left in the world. Determined to find out what happened to all the others, she sets off on a quest to find and ultimately rescue them.

2. *Phoebe and Her Unicorn* (2012)

A collection of comics by Dana Simpson, *Phoebe and Her Unicorn* features—you guessed it!—a human girl named Phoebe and her very unusual best friend: Marigold the unicorn. When Marigold has to grant Phoebe a wish the first time they meet, Phoebe wishes for them to be best friends. Together, the two confront typical childhood dramas like frenemies, babysitting, and back-to-school blues with grace and humor. Best of all, because Marigold lives in Phoebe's human world, there's a unicorn on every page of this lighthearted comic collection.

And if this book leaves you looking for more, you don't need to stop reading. It's just the first in a long series of books, and you can also follow the comic online, one strip at a time.

3. *Into the Land of the Unicorns* (1994)

If one unicorn isn't enough for you, how about a land ruled by them? *Into the Land of the Unicorns* is the first book of a series that takes place in the magical land of Luster. Written by Bruce Coville, the first book follows Cara, a girl whose grandmother tells her to leap from a clock tower while wearing a magical amulet. She leaps—but doesn't land in the church square. Instead, Cara finds herself in a completely different world—one that she must fight to save.

Cara's adventures in Luster are full of suspense, adventure, and fantastic creatures, and they don't end with the book. There are three more books in this series, called the Unicorn Chronicles, to keep the unicorn magic going.

4. The Unicorn in the Barn (2017)

For anyone who's ever imagined tucking a unicorn into their barn and caring for it, Jacqueline Ogburn's *The Unicorn in the Barn* is a dream come true. When eleven-year-old Eric Harper goes looking for a mysterious white deer, he catches a glimpse of it in the woods—but knows that it's no deer. It shimmers softly in the light, and has a single horn curving from its forehead. Eric realizes that he's seen a unicorn, and later discovers that his neighbors, a veterinarian and her daughter, are caring for it.

5. Nico Bravo and the Hound of Hades (2019)

Not every unicorn is beautiful. Not every unicorn is graceful. Buck, the unicorn in Mike Cavallaro's graphic novel *Nico Bravo and the Hound of Hades*, is neither. Nico Bravo is a boy who works at Vulcan's Celestial Supply Shop, an outfitter for mythical gods and monsters. His world is filled with legendary creatures, so it's not so surprising that he barely notices his coworker Buck, a unicorn whose horn has been bent through years of fighting in the Unicorn Wars. Buck walks on his hind legs, wears a vest and a bandanna headband, and is ready to whip out his karate moves on a moment's notice. He's definitely a unicorn of a different kind, but he plays an important part in Nico's quest.

6. The Transfigured Hart (1975)

Richard and Heather, two teenagers, have very different ways of looking at the world. Richard is lonely and isolated. Heather is a popular girl. But they both love to explore the woods. One day, they each stumble across an unusual animal there. Near a shimmering pool, they find a hart—a type of deer—that is completely white. Or is it? Heather believes it is, but romantic Richard is sure that it's a unicorn. They both agree that they must protect it, since deer-hunting season is about to begin. As they race to save the mysterious animal, Richard begins to convince Heather of his point of view, until they finally share an encounter with the unicorn in the woods.

7. *A Swiftly Tilting Planet* (1978)

Unicorns and science fiction don't often mix, so when one does appear in a sci-fi/fantasy book, it's an opportunity you shouldn't miss. *A Swiftly Tilting Planet*, the third book in Madeleine L'Engle's classic Time Quintet series, begins with Charles Wallace, the story's hero, visiting a stargazing spot near his home. While he's there, a winged unicorn named Gaudior appears and tells him that he must travel through time to prevent the outbreak of a nuclear war. While Charles Wallace must do the hard work, Gaudior travels with Charles Wallace and guides him, visiting every chapter as he helps to save the world.

8. *The Little White Horse* (1946)

When thirteen-year-old Maria Merriweather's father dies, she is sent to live with her cousin in a mysterious manor in the country. The ancient estate is romantic and beautiful and steeped in magic. Exploring its grounds, Maria finds ancient tunnels, tiny doors, and beautifully carved ceilings, along with an ancient mystery, a magical lion, and a little white horse that turns out to be a unicorn. Elizabeth Goudge wrote *The Little White Horse* during World War II but set it one hundred years earlier. Even though the unicorn in the book is mostly glimpsed from afar, it is still the perfect read for anyone who loves to see candlelight, long dresses, Victorian romance, and breathtaking scenery alongside their magic.

9. *The Last Battle* (1956)

C. S. Lewis's Chronicles of Narnia series is hailed as one of the great literary works of the twentieth century. A sweeping fantasy, it tells of a magical world called Narnia and the good and evil forces that clash to rule it. The final book of the series, *The Last Battle,* includes a unicorn named Jewel who serves as the right-hand man and friend of King Tirian.

Jewel only makes a few appearances in the book, but he's a memorable character. Like all the animals in Narnia, he can talk, and he's a steady voice of reason when much of Narnia seems to be going mad. While Jewel isn't the only unicorn to appear in the series (Peter Pevensie rides one into battle in the first book of the series, *The Lion, the Witch and the Wardrobe*), he is the one with by far the most personality, and is worth getting to know.

10. *Through the Looking Glass* (1871)

A unicorn makes one of the first appearances in modern literature in Lewis Carroll's classic fantasy about a girl named Alice who passes into the fantastic world through a mirror. While the unicorn makes a fairly short appearance (during which he mostly argues with his nemesis, the lion) he does manage to impart some unicorniness, and to coin a classic line: "Well, now that we have seen each other," he tells Alice, "if you'll believe in me, I'll believe in you."

UNICORNS AT THE MOVIES

What's the next best thing to seeing a unicorn in person? Watching one on the big screen! Thanks to the magic of CGI and animation, unicorns have been frolicking through cinema for decades. Unicorns in the movies run the gambit from wild mustangs who happen to have horns to talking ponies with party-planning problems. Try one of these movies, ranked here by unicorniness, the next time you're hunting for a unicorn.

1. *The Last Unicorn* (1982)

Directed by Jules Bass and Arthur Rankin Jr., this animated film is as popular as the classic fantasy book it was based on. It features an all-star voice cast, with the actress Mia Farrow voicing the graceful, long-legged unicorn, and a script written by the author of the book, Peter Beagle.

2. *My Little Pony: The Movie* (2017)

You can't get more pop-culture-unicorny than this! Since Hasbro first introduced unicorn ponies, My Little Pony has added more and more to their stable. The My Little Pony movie stars flying unicorn Twilight Sparkle and her pony friends as they fight to save their homeland from invasion by the evil Storm King.

3. *Nico the Unicorn* (1998)

Another great story for anyone who fantasizes about keeping a unicorn as a pet, *Nico the Unicorn* tells the story of Billy, a boy who rescues a pony from a circus and discovers that it is pregnant with a unicorn foal. Once the residents of his small Vermont town learn what he's keeping in his barn, Billy has to save the unicorn by riding it on a wild chase to freedom.

4. *The Fantastic Adventures of Unico* (1981)

This funky anime from the '80s stars what is definitely the cutest unicorn you'll ever see. Unico is a round-faced, big-eyed unicorn foal, whose magical power is that he makes everyone happy. This isn't okay with the gods, who separate Unico from his family, setting him on an adorable adventure.

Video Games

The only thing better than watching a unicorn on the screen is getting to *interact* with a unicorn on the screen. (That, or getting to meet a real unicorn, but that's a whole other adventure—see page 99 to learn about unicorn tracking.) Unicorns can be found in all kinds of video games, from virtual reality to puzzle and open-world games. Here are five of the most talked-about unicorn games from the twenty-first century:

1. *Robot Unicorn Attack* (2010)
   You're the attacking robot in this arcade-style game, which lets you run full speed with all the power and magic of a unicorn, all while listening to some fantastic '80s tunes.

2. *Secret of the Magic Crystals* (2010)
   Players run a horse stable, breeding, caring for, and training horses in this fantasy game. Along with regular horses, you can raise flying horses and unicorns, too!

3. *The Unicorn Princess* (2019)
   In this open-world game for very young players, the horse and rider transform into a unicorn and a princess—and back again.

4. *The Sims* 3: *Pets* (2011)
   Gamers in the know can add a unicorn to their Sims family with this add-on pack. But you'll have to make friends with your unicorn and meet its special requirements first.

5. *Peggle* (2007)
   A puzzle game that challenges players to clear pegs off a board by shooting a ball at them, *Peggle* features several animals, including Bjorn the unicorn, head of the Peggle Institute.

5. *Legend* (1985)

If you want to see gorgeous, realistic unicorns frolicking in a magical forest, then you'll love this live-action film, made by Ridley Scott at the height of the '80s unicorn craze. Tom Cruise and Mia Sara star in this dark fantasy about a princess and a forest dweller who must battle the Prince of Darkness to save a unicorn and release the kingdom from a magical winter.

6. *The Little Unicorn* (2001)

Polly Regan is an orphan who lives a carefree life on a farm with her grandfather. That is, until her favorite horse gives birth to a baby unicorn. Polly bonds with the little unicorn and takes care of it, but stories about the foal get out and people come from all over to see it. When the unicorn is stolen by an unscrupulous circus owner, Polly must run away and rescue it.

7. *The Secret of Moonacre* (2008)

Based on Elizabeth Goudge's book *The Little White Horse*, this live-action film stays pretty true to the original. It follows the story of Maria Merryweather as she gets to the bottom of a family curse at Moonacre Manor. Along with the lion that protects the family, you can see the unicorn in the flesh.

8. *Unicorn Store* (2019)

This very modern take on unicorns brings them into our world. Kit, played by Brie Larson, is having a hard time fitting into adult life and finds herself at a magical store. The store's salesman tells her that he can sell her a unicorn. But she'll have to go through a series of tasks to get ready for it first. Although the unicorn itself is only glimpsed toward the end, the film is steeped in unicorniness, with rainbows and glitter at every turn.

9. *Stardust* (2007)

A sweeping live-action fantasy, *Stardust* features an all-star cast and a big budget. It follows a young man, Tristan, on his quest to capture a fallen star. The star, as it turns out, is a woman named Yvaine. The fallen star gallops through the story on unicorn-back, and while the unicorn may not be a central character, the movie's worth a watch to see the unicorn battle an evil witch and her henchmen.

10. *The Lion, the Witch and the Wardrobe* (2005)

You can catch glimpses of a unicorn in the live-action film version of C. S. Lewis's classic *The Lion, the Witch and the Wardrobe*. This is the first story in the Chronicles of Narnia series, in which Lucy, Susan, Edmund, and Peter fight to save Narnia from the White Witch. Peter rides a unicorn into the epic battle at the end of the movie.

ᴜNISTARS

Today's unicorn characters brim over with personality. They're trusty steeds to their human companions, are reliable friends to other animals, and go on their own adventures. Here are just a few of the unicorns who have captured hearts in the last fifty years—and helped bring unicorns from supporting roles into the spotlight.

BUTTERCUP

If there's one thing that holds true of twenty-first-century unicorns, it's that they come in *all* shapes and sizes. Need evidence? How about Buttercup, the stuffed unicorn in Pixar's animated Toy Story movies? Buttercup may be made of plush and stuffing, but he's all unicorn—even if his nostrils are made of hearts.

SWIFT WIND

When Filmation launched the Saturday-morning cartoon character She-Ra in 1983, they also introduced her fierce battle steed, Swift Wind. A feisty white stallion with a golden horn, orange mane and tail, and rainbow wings, Swift Wind can talk—and he definitely has opinions. The series was relaunched in 2018 by DreamWorks, and Swift Wind got an even bigger dose of personality.

UNICO

Cuteness incarnate, Unico embodies the pop-culture ideal of unicorns as creatures of joy and light. Full of magic that he doesn't yet understand, Unico has a decidedly babylike personality and appeal. But when the chips are down, he transforms into a full-sized, winged unicorn to rescue those he loves.

THE UNICORN/LADY AMALTHEA

You may have noticed that *The Last Unicorn* appears again and again on these lists of unicorn literature, movies, and characters. Yes—it's that important to the pop unicorn story. The movie's heroine may have done more than any other single unicorn to establish the idea of unicorns as creatures with personality and drive. Soft-spoken and gentle, she nevertheless has the mettle to fight for those she loves—and for all unicornkind.

TWILIGHT SPARKLE

My Little Pony has created dozens of unicorns over the years and has probably added more to the world of pop-culture unicorns than any other brand. Among the hundreds of ponies they've created as toys and animated characters, there have been winged ponies and fifty or so unicorns. All the My Little Pony characters have distinct personalities, mostly defined by their hobbies and their "cutie marks"—symbols on their flank that represent them.

Twilight Sparkle, with her lavender coat, blue-and-pink mane, and star cutie mark, pranced onto the scene in 2010. A bookish unicorn who loves the library and studies magic, she's the heroine of the Friendship Is Magic series, as well as two My Little Pony movies. Twilight Sparkle gained wings when she became Princess of Equestria.

Name Your Own Unicorn

Have you ever noticed that the names of a lot of pop-culture unicorns sound kind of similar? They seem to follow a certain formula. It goes something like this: adjective + light effect = unicorn name. It's not an exact science; you can sub in a noun from the natural world for either variable, or reverse the order, and come up with a perfectly passable pony name. Try it yourself—combine any two words from the columns below, or add your own.

ADJECTIVE	NATURE ELEMENT	LIGHT EFFECT
Bright	Rainbow	Shimmer
Shining	Cloud	Glitter
Gentle	Storm	Shadow
Super	Wind	Shine
Radiant	Dawn	Dance
Wise	Star	Light
Brave	Rain	Glimmer
Brilliant	Moon	Twinkle

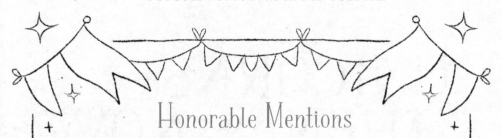

Honorable Mentions

UNIKITTY

In the 2010s, unicorns broke out of the horse mold and began to appear in all kinds of different shapes and sizes. The 2014 Lego movie included Unikitty, a relentlessly positive pink cat with a spiraling blue horn on her forehead. Like any cat, Unikitty could be a ferocious fighter, too. Her sweet and sassy character took off and inspired a Unikitty TV show in 2017.

STARLITE

In the midst of the 1980s unicorn craze, a TV show called *Rainbow Brite* appeared. A redheaded girl with a bubbly personality and distinctly '80s boots and shoulder pads, Rainbow Brite had a magical belt that brought color and cheer to the universe. Rainbow Brite's faithful steed was a flying horse named Starlite, who stopped just short of being a unicorn. A white stallion with golden hooves and a rainbow mane and tail, Starlite sported a bright yellow star on his forehead instead of a horn.

UNICORNS— THEN AND NOW

- 398 BCE Ctesias puts the finishing touches on a book that describes a unicorn as a white donkey with a dark red head, dark blue eyes, and a tricolored horn.

- CA. 53 BCE Julius Caesar describes a stag with a single horn that lives in the Hercynian Forest.

- 79 CE Pliny the Elder's unicorn has an elephant's feet, a horse's body, a stag's head, and a tricolored horn.

- 2ND CENTURY The *Physiologus* is compiled in Alexandria, Egypt.

- 3RD CENTURY The unicorn has a tawny coat and a mane. Its horn grows to three feet and gains rings in a description written by Aelian.

- 4TH CENTURY Julius Solinus describes an animal with a four-foot-long horn of "wonderful brightness." Incredibly fierce, it cannot be taken alive.

550 An Egyptian merchant named Cosmas Indicoplesutis creates the first known drawing of a unicorn, based on statues he saw in Ethiopia. It is a powerful animal with a bearded, goatlike head; a long, straight horn; a bronze coat; and clawlike feet.

12TH CENTURY King William of Scotland adds the unicorn to the country's coat of arms.

1224 Genghis Khan decides not to invade India after encountering a unicorn that bows to him three times.

1468 The wedding banquet of Princess Margaret to the Duke of Burgundy is decorated with at least five massive alicorns.

1484 King James III of Scotland mints *unicornis*—gold coins stamped with a unicorn.

1495 The unicorn tapestries are begun in the Netherlands.

1539 Friar Marcus of Nizza encounters a unicorn hide near Mexico. It is "half as big again as the hide of an ox, with one horn on his forehead, bending toward the breast."

1564 Sir John Hawkins reports that native Floridians wear beads of unicorn horn around their necks.

1584 Emperor Theodore Ivanovitch is crowned in Moscow while holding a jewel-encrusted imperial staff made from an "alicorn."

1603 The unicorn joins the lion on the coat of arms of Great Britain.

1611 A new translation of the Bible is published at the command of King James I of England. Scholars translate the Hebrew word *re'em* as *unicorn*. Unicorns appear seven times in the new translation.

1612 Dutch cartographer Jacob Bartsch adds the constellation "Monoceros Unicornis" to a globe, popularizing a new constellation shaped like a unicorn.

1671 Christian V is crowned king of Denmark and Norway while sitting on a throne made of "alicorn." (Twentieth-century tests will later reveal it to be narwhal tusk.)

1673 Dr. Olfert Dapper discovers unicorns along the Canadian border. They resemble horses but with cloven hooves, rough manes, curled tails like a wild boar, black eyes, necks like those of stags, and, of course, a "long, straight horn upon the forehead."

1801 Sir John Barrow reports a cave painting of a unicorn in South Africa. The *Encyclopaedia Britannica* insists that unicorns must exist there.

LATE 1800s Most naturalists have given up on the hope of finding a unicorn and decide that they must be entirely mythical.

1871 Lewis Carroll includes a unicorn in his classic children's book *Through the Looking Glass.*

1963 British country-rock band Unicorn is formed. They will eventually release five albums.

1968 Peter Beagle pens the classic fantasy *The Last Unicorn*.

1980s Unicorns become a fashion craze, appearing on T-shirts, lunchboxes, and camper vans.

1984 My Little Pony takes unicorns to the next level with toys and a TV series.

1985 Ringling Bros. and Barnum and Bailey circus sparks controversy when it begins to tour with a "unicorn" named Lancelot. (He's actually a goat whose horn buds were sewn together when he was a kid.)

2010 My Little Pony reboots with *My Little Pony: Friendship Is Magic* and starts a new craze for unicorn ponies. The mania spreads to young men, and "bronies" are born.

2013 Venture capitalist Eileen Lee uses the term "unicorn" to describe start-up businesses with a value of more than $1 billion, creating a new use for the word.

2017 Unicornimania resurges, leading to the creation of the Starbucks unicorn frappuccino, unicorn "snot" body glitter, and giant unicorn-shaped pool floats.

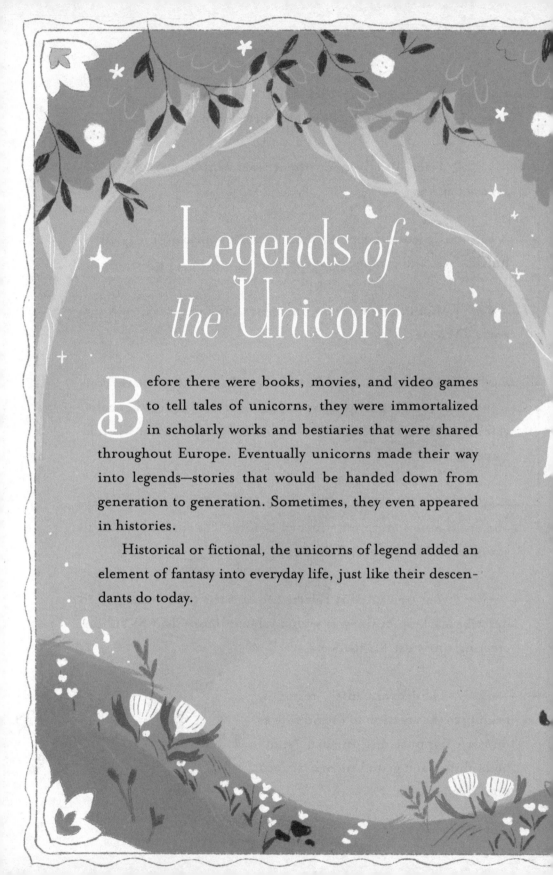

Legends of the Unicorn

Before there were books, movies, and video games to tell tales of unicorns, they were immortalized in scholarly works and bestiaries that were shared throughout Europe. Eventually unicorns made their way into legends—stories that would be handed down from generation to generation. Sometimes, they even appeared in histories.

Historical or fictional, the unicorns of legend added an element of fantasy into everyday life, just like their descendants do today.

THE BESTIARY

Medieval bestiaries formed the basis for most of unicorn legend in Europe, and they told two basic stories. Most simply tell the story of how the unicorn is captured or killed when it falls for a maiden, laying its head in her lap so that the hunters can leap out and seize it. But the Greek bestiary tells a tale that pits the unicorn, a symbol of God, against the serpent, a stand-in for Satan . . .

There was once a traveler, a weary man who had walked all day and for many days before that with all his possessions rolled up in a pack on his back. There was nothing terribly remarkable about this man. Except, perhaps, that he was observant. That would soon save his skin.

After a long and tiring day walking in the hot sun, he came across a glade with spreading shade trees and a glittering spring. His feet and back were aching, and he hadn't had fresh water in days, so he joyfully threw down his pack and made for the water's edge. When he got there, he dipped one hand in, scooping up water to drink. But then something made him pause.

In the cup of his hand, the water looked inviting, but as he raised it toward his mouth, he saw that the surface of the water swirled with an oily rainbow. He was so thirsty and the water looked so inviting, but he reconsidered his drink. He dropped it back into the spring and wiped his hand on his breeches. He promised himself that he would have some soon. But first he set his back against a tree trunk to watch the glade and see what happened. It wasn't long before he dozed off.

Hours later, he was startled awake by a sound. The sun had given way to night. His arms and legs ached with the strain of travel and his mouth was dry as sawdust, but that wasn't what had woken him up. He strained his ears for a moment and heard a soft rustling in the bushes to his right.

There was a swish of movement. He blinked the sleep from his eyes and stared into the bushes, then at the trees around them. He finally saw it on the ground by the spring: a serpent. Black as the night around it, it was more of a shadow than a snake. But it moved with the strength and flow of a snake. It was ten feet long, powerful and deadly.

When the serpent reached the spring, it raised its diamond-shaped head and then leaned out over the water. The man leaned out, too, straining in the dark to see what it was doing. It opened its mouth, letting loose a stream of venom that spread out over the pool like an oil slick. Then it quietly turned and slithered away.

The man swallowed, grateful that he hadn't taken a drink earlier. He resolved to leave the next morning without touching the water. Then he spent an uneasy night, worried that the serpent might return. He finally drifted back to sleep in the early hours of the morning.

Again, he was awakened by a rustling in the bushes. This time, it was harmless: A rabbit loped out of the bushes and stopped at the edge of the spring. It did not drink but sat patiently as though it were waiting for something. A few minutes later, a deer slipped from the trees behind him and took its place next to the rabbit. They were followed by a flock of birds who perched in the trees, a boar, a fox, and a stately bear. None of the animals threatened any of the others, and none touched the water. They simply sat, patient and still, as though they were waiting for something.

The man sat, rooted to his spot. He was unsure what to do next, overwhelmed with curiosity about what it was the animals could be waiting for. He wasn't in suspense for long. When the last of the dawn faded and the sky was a brilliant blue, a unicorn arrived. It walked slowly and sedately past the line of woodland creatures, bobbing its head at each, then approached the poisoned pool.

It gestured over the waters briefly, then dipped its horn gently in. Then it took a long, deep drink. One by one, the animals followed, glugging giant stomachfuls before wandering back the way they had come. When all the woodland animals had left the glade, the unicorn followed them, leaving the man entirely alone.

He crawled hesitantly toward the pool and dipped in one hand. Raising the water to the light, he realized that it was no longer oily. The serpent's poison had been completely neutralized. He took a tenuous sip. The water was sweet, cool, and pure. He dropped his face to the water's surface and took great gulps of it. The ache left his legs. He felt like he had many weeks ago, before he had started his journey—strong and energetic and ready for anything.

Picking up his pack, he said a quiet thank-you to the unicorn and continued on his way.

GENGHIS KHAN

Genghis Khan was one of the greatest—and most feared—men in history. His tactical genius set the Mongolian people on a path to building an enormous empire, one that would overrun an entire continent. So it's only natural that his story has blurred into legend. And perhaps it's not so very surprising that the legends of Genghis included an encounter with a powerful magical beast: a unicorn.

When Genghis Khan was born in a yurt on the wild grasslands of Mongolia, no one could have known that he would become a great leader—although later people would insist there had been auspicious signs pointing to his destiny. At the time, Mongolia was not a united country. Nomadic tribes lived on the steppes, each loyal to their own small group. They moved with the seasons, battling and forming alliances with other tribes in a constantly shifting landscape.

He was named Temujin, and he did not have a happy childhood. His father died when he was nine, and his tribe rejected his family, leaving them unprotected. He was captured into slavery and escaped. Then he killed his own half brother to gain control of the family. Over time, he built an army, based on a clever idea. Until then, tribal leaders had given out positions of rank based on family ties and alliances. Temujin had had enough of family ties—he gathered men around him based on their abilities.

By 1206, Mongolia had been united into one empire, and Temujin had become Genghis Khan (*Khan* means "ruler" or "great leader"). He began to look elsewhere for conquests.

The soldiers in Genghis Khan's army were unusually skilled. Centuries of life on the steppes had made them excellent horsemen. Hunting from horseback in wide-open spaces had sharpened their archery skills. Their specialized bows could fire an arrow more than a thousand feet, and they rode with stirrups, a relatively new invention that left their hands free to use their weapons. They were loyal to their leader, who promised them promotion in the ranks based on their performance in battle.

And they had a reputation for ruthlessness. The Mongol army swept in on armored horseback, firing a hail of arrows with deadly precision. They killed anyone in their path and burned whole cities to the ground. They were so ferocious that when they moved into the lands of the neighboring Jin dynasty, they conquered an army ten times their size. Since the Mongols were nomadic, they kept moving forward from one conquest to the next, taking what they wanted.

By 1224, the Mongol Empire stretched from the east coast of Asia, across what is now China and Tibet, and west to the Caspian Sea. Genghis Khan then turned his eyes toward his neighbors to the south and advanced his armies to the borders of the Delhi Sultanate (modern-day India).

The army reached the Iron Pass, a route through the mountains near the edge of the Sultanate, and advanced to its top. From there they would be able to see the lands below and the possibilities for plunder. Genghis Khan rode his mare at the front of the army, eager to see his next conquest. But when he arrived at the top of the pass, he found something he had not expected. There, an animal waited for him.

It was shaped like a deer, with the tail of a horse and a single horn on its forehead. It stood there with purpose, not in the least intimidated by the sea of horses and men that approached. The army came to a halt.

For a moment, Genghis looked curiously at the strange animal. Then he dismounted and approached it on foot. When he was just a few feet away from the animal, it stretched one leg out in front and bowed low. It rose to its feet and bowed again—three times in all. But it did not move out of the army's path. Genghis believed in signs and portents, and he knew one when he saw it. It was clear that the unicorn was telling him something. The army settled in for the night while the great khan brooded.

By morning, he had an answer: The unicorn could only have been the spirit of his father, come to warn him. The army could not advance through the pass, and they could not take India. Heeding the warning, they pulled up stakes and headed back the way they came.

We'll never know whether Genghis Khan was right about what the unicorn meant (or whether the unicorn was right to warn him off). But the Mongol Empire continued to flourish even after Genghis Khan's death. It became the largest contiguous empire in the history of the world, swallowing all of Asia and much of the Middle East and Eastern Europe, too.

But it never conquered India.

RHIANNON

The tale of Rhiannon and her unicorn is told throughout the British Isles. In some versions she is Celtic, in others she's British. But a few things always remain the same. Rhiannon is always "orphaned" by the wicked Sir Brangwyn, who takes her parents away from her. She searches for truffles with the help of a very unlikely truffle hunter. And the story never, ever ends well for Sir Brangwyn.

More than a thousand years ago, among the gentle, rolling hills of Wales, there lived a girl named Rhiannon. She was a strong child, and brave. Her strength had come from the hard work of village life. Her bravery she had inherited from her father. He was never afraid to stand up for what was right and often protested against the hefty taxes that the local lord demanded.

Back then, villagers didn't own their tidy little houses, the land that they lived on, or even the vegetables they grew in their gardens.

Everything for miles around—everything that Rhiannon had ever laid her eyes on—belonged to Sir Brangwyn, the nobleman who lived in the nearby castle. Every year, Sir Brangwyn demanded more and more from his serfs, which meant that less and less of the food that they grew went into their own stomachs. In the summer months, when their gardens were bursting with food and chickens wandered through the village, the people who lived there scraped by. But in the winter, when the fields lay fallow, they had nothing to eat. All their stores had been whisked away to the castle to satisfy the enormous appetites of Sir Brangwyn.

It was in the middle of one of those winters, when the land was brown and bare and the cold wind rattled the stalks in the fields, that the knights arrived to take Rhiannon's father away. Sir Brangwyn had grown weary of his complaints, so the lord accused him of poaching and had him dragged to the castle dungeon. His wife, Rhiannon's mother, was forced to go, too. She would have to work in the castle kitchen or her husband would not be fed. Nine-year-old Rhiannon was left to fend for herself.

As the winter wore on, Rhiannon grew thinner and thinner. Her neighbors were not unkind—they shared the warmth of their homes and kept her company, but they hardly had food to keep their own children alive, never mind an extra. So the girl drifted from house to house to scrabble together a living.

Winter warmed to muddy spring and the trees and fields began to show tinges of green. Then summer arrived with the promise of food for everyone. Rhiannon knew she would need to take advantage of the warm months to provide for herself if she was going to survive much longer on her own, but what could one slight and hungry girl do? She couldn't push a plow or carry enough water to tend a field. But like everyone else in the village, she would have to pay the lord and earn her right to live there.

Rhiannon had nothing to give to the castle by way of taxes. But there was one thing that Sir Brangwyn prized and could not get his hands on. He longed for truffles, rare and delicious mushrooms that were devilishly tricky to find. They grew in the forest in summer, among the roots of the oak trees, buried beneath the ground.

If you have ever tried to find something that's hidden underground, you know that it's not an easy task. Even if you know which kind of tree the truffles preferred, there's no guarantee that there's a truffle under any given tree. And even if there is a truffle there, there's still an awful lot of dirt beneath the average oak tree, and a lot of digging to do before you can find what you're looking for. All this meant that, although Sir Brangwyn had truffle hunters galore, he didn't have any truffles in his pantry.

Rhiannon had no idea how to find truffles, of course, but she was a strong and brave girl, so she gathered a basket and her rough woolen cloak and headed to the forest outside the village. The woods there were dark and deep, and the high branches groaned and creaked in the wind.

But they were also full of life. Cheerful birds hopped from tree to tree, squirrels scuttled across the canopy, and a little brook flowed noisily through. Rhiannon felt at home there and sang all day as she worked her way from tree to tree, digging hopefully under one after another. She sang through the first day as the sun filtered through the trees, and through the second, when a thick fog rolled in from the Celtic Sea. Once or twice, she heard the rustling of a bigger animal—a deer or boar, she thought—moving nearby, and she stopped to listen. But nothing appeared, and so she sang on.

Three days passed this way, and then a fourth. But when the sun began to set on the fifth day and Rhiannon's basket was still empty, she finally sat down and cried. She was a strong girl, and a brave girl, but she was also tired and hungry. Her fingers were cracked and sore and caked with dirt, and in five days of searching she hadn't found a single truffle. And so she sat, crumpled in a heap below a spreading oak tree, and sobbed. She only stopped when she heard the sound again—the snap of a twig, the rustle of leaves. And then something stepped out of the brush.

It wasn't a deer or a boar at all, but a creature covered in downy white hair from head to toe. Its head and body looked like a horse's, but its toes were cloven like a goat's. Its legs were so long and gangly and its mane and tail so short that Rhiannon realized, all in a rush, that it was a baby. That also explained why the horn that spiraled from its forehead was only a few inches long.

The unicorn foal walked warily past her to a patch of earth between the roots of the tree and began to paw the ground. Rhiannon just stared with her mouth open, even when it looked her in the eye and, slowly and deliberately, turned toward the tree roots and pawed the ground again.

It took three tries before she understood.

"Are you trying to help?" she asked it. "But there's nothing under that tree. I've looked, and there's nothing there."

The unicorn did not agree. It pawed the ground with such determination, and snorted with such frustration that she finally knelt on the ground between its hooves and began to dig. She easily scooped big handfuls of the soft black dirt until she had dug so far that she was up to her wrists. There at the bottom of the hole, instead of loose dirt, her fingers scraped against something bumpy.

Rhiannon's heart beat faster. She carefully dug around the object and pulled it out. It was the size of an apple, round and black, its surface covered in pits and grooves like a lump of charcoal—a truffle, and a big one.

Rhiannon threw her arms around the foal's neck and buried her face in its brush-bristle mane. "Thank you," she said.

The foal did not object. It stayed put while she hugged it, and waited patiently by as she picked up her basket and tied on her woolen cloak. Then it followed her amiably back through the trees until she reached the edge of the forest. As Rhiannon stepped out of the woods, the foal disappeared into the trees. And, although she was sorry to see it go, she set off for the castle cheerful at the prospect of food.

The yeoman at the gate moved quickly when he saw what was in Rhiannon's basket, snatching it up greedily and telling her to wait. He scuttled in through the great stone archway of the castle and returned a few moments later to lead her into the great hall, where Sir Brangwyn sat at a heavy oak table.

"You brought this?" he asked, gesturing with a fork to Rhiannon's basket, which sat on the table next to his plate.

Rhiannon squared her shoulders. "Yes."

Sir Brangwyn fixed her with his beady eyes. He did not like her defiant nature. "A truffle like this," he said, "is worth a lot. I would give you a sack of grain for it, but it is obvious that you stole it. Tell me where you stole it from, and I'll let you go free."

"I didn't steal it," Rhiannon answered calmly. "I found it."

"I have dozens of truffle hunters who search every day. They haven't brought me a truffle this big in years. How could you possibly have found it, when they could not?"

Rhiannon shrugged. "I know a place."

Sir Brangwyn considered his options. He didn't believe that this little girl could possibly have found such an enormous, rare truffle on her own. He was inclined to throw her in the dungeon with her troublesome father. But the villagers would surely object to him locking away a young girl, so he decided he needed to prove his case first.

"Very well," he said smugly. "If you know a place, then surely you can find me another. Come back tomorrow with a truffle larger than this one, and I'll give you two sacks of grain. But if you fail to bring me another truffle, I'll know that you stole this one, and I'll have you thrown in the dungeon."

Of course, Rhiannon had no idea how she would find another

truffle. But she really didn't have much choice, and two whole sacks of grain would feed her for months. So she agreed.

The next morning, Rhiannon took her basket and her cloak and went back to the deep, dark woods. They had begun to feel like home to her, and she sang a cheerful song as she walked. Before long, there was a rustling of leaves, and the unicorn foal appeared. It did not waste time, but took her straight to the roots of a gnarled white oak where Rhiannon dug up a truffle as big as a grapefruit. They spent the rest of the afternoon playing, with the unicorn leaping and running like a puppy and wagging its tail when she scratched its neck. When it was time to return to the village, the little white foal followed Rhiannon to the edge of the wood, then disappeared when she stepped out of the trees.

The yeoman at the castle gate didn't even try to hide his amazement when Rhiannon arrived with her truffle that night. He immediately led her to the great hall, where Sir Brangwyn was seated at the oaken table. The lord looked up from his plate and set down his fork. "You found another," he said.

"Yes," Rhiannon replied simply. She may have smiled just a bit.

Sir Brangwyn was stuck. He hated to reward any of his serfs, but even an evil, selfish lord had to follow certain rules. He could hardly throw Rhiannon into the dungeon after she had done what he asked.

"Very well," he said. "You shall have your grain." Then he had another idea. "Bring me another tomorrow, bigger than this one, and I will take it in payment for the village taxes."

Rhiannon readily agreed to the deal. All she needed was one

more truffle, and she could repay the villagers for sheltering her through the winter.

As she ran out of the castle gate and down the village road, Sir Brangwyn called in the yeoman and gave him an order. "Tomorrow morning, go down to the village and follow Rhiannon into the woods—but don't let her see you. Find out how she is getting these truffles."

The next day, Rhiannon went to the woods once again. The yeoman had arrived that morning with two heavy bags of grain, and Rhiannon was feeling quite cheerful as she set out. She sang as she crossed from the fields into the forest and had not gone more than a few feet beneath the trees before the unicorn appeared. She could tell that it was quite pleased with itself as it led her to an ancient beech tree, dancing and tossing its head before it pawed the earth beneath it. There, Rhiannon found a truffle as big as a watermelon. It was so big it barely fit into her basket. After she had dug it up, Rhiannon and the unicorn played for hours, hiding among the tree trunks and napping together on the soft moss. Neither saw the yeoman, who watched Rhiannon dig up her treasure and skulked back to the castle to report on what he had seen.

When it was time for Rhiannon to leave, the foal disappeared once again at the edge of the woods, and once again, the girl headed straight for the castle with her incredible mushroom.

When the yeoman led Rhiannon into the great hall that night, she thought he seemed slower and more tired than he had been the day before. And when she showed him her astonishingly large truffle, he wasn't the slightest bit surprised by it.

In the great hall, Sir Brangwyn was ready for her. The table was empty, except for the basket and its truffle. He was quite pleased with the news the yeoman had given him earlier that day. He was an avid hunter but had never managed to kill a unicorn. So imagine his delight at finding that there was one in his very own woods.

"Your secret is out," he said. "I know about the unicorn."

Rhiannon's heart skipped a beat, but she held her ground.

"What unicorn?" she asked.

Sir Brangwyn leaned in close. "The unicorn," he said, his face inches from hers, "that showed you where to find that truffle."

Sir Brangwyn didn't have any patience for peasants, and he was already weary of dealing with this one. But he was also a man who knew a thing or two about unicorns. If he wanted to kill one, he would need Rhiannon's help.

"I will make this very easy for you," he said. "Tomorrow, we will go to the woods. You will call the unicorn. Once I have killed it, I will set your father free. How does that sound?"

Rhiannon wanted nothing more than to free her father from Sir Brangwyn's dungeons, but she could not give up the unicorn. She stared blankly back at Sir Brangwyn and said again, "What unicorn?"

But Sir Brangwyn was very used to getting what he wanted, and he was very resourceful when it came to convincing others to give it to him. He chuckled. "If I do not kill the unicorn, I can promise you that your father will not leave the dungeons alive."

Poor Rhiannon. She loved the unicorn and knew that without it she would surely have starved. But she loved her father, too, and couldn't bear to be the cause of his death. So when Sir Brangwyn and two knights arrived in the village the next morning, she picked up her basket and her cloak and she headed toward the forest. As she stepped into the trees, Sir Brangwyn and the knights hung back to wait for the unicorn to come. When it had arrived and laid its head on Rhiannon's lap, they would leap out and kill it. Until then, they hid in a thicket of laurel, the knights with their bows at the ready and Sir Brangwyn with his spear.

Rhiannon walked quietly through the woods. She couldn't bring herself to sing, and the foal did not appear. She couldn't disguise her relief hours later, when Sir Brangwyn grew weary of sitting on the cold ground and told his knights it was time to head home. They put their arrows in their quivers and stretched their arms and legs, stiff from sitting so quietly for hours, and left the forest. Rhiannon stayed behind, weeping from relief. She did not realize that Sir Brangwyn had doubled back and crept behind a nearby rock. She only knew that she—and the unicorn—had made it through another day.

When she felt certain that the knights had gone, she spread out her cloak beneath a yew tree, sat down, and began to sing to herself. It wasn't a joyful song, like the ones she had sung just a few days earlier. It was slow and melancholy and sweet. Almost immediately, the little foal appeared. It wagged its tail agreeably at the sound of her voice and skipped a few steps from the very same laurel bushes that the hunting party had been hiding in an hour earlier.

Sir Brangwyn sprang from his hiding place behind the rock, his dagger raised and ready to fly.

But before he could take a step toward the little foal, the sound of hoofbeats filled the wood. In a flash of white, a unicorn soared over the rock and landed, head down, on the other side. This was

no foal. It towered over Sir Brangwyn, as large as a carthorse. Its horn, almost three feet long, spiraled to a vicious point. It took just seconds for the unicorn to finish off the lord with that lethal horn before it galloped on, leaving Rhiannon and the foal behind.

Of course, everyone waited for Sir Brangwyn to return. Days passed, and then weeks. Eventually it was very clear that the lord would not be coming home. I can't say that anyone in the village was sorry to hear that Sir Brangwyn was gone. Certainly none of them asked too many questions about what had happened to him.

A villager had seen Rhiannon coming out of the woods the evening that Sir Brangwyn disappeared. She had stopped at the edge of the trees and looked back for a moment. The villager could have sworn that he saw a small white animal with her, a deer, or maybe a goat. Rhiannon had kissed it fondly on its nose before it sprang away into the woods, and she had turned toward home. But surely that tiny, goatlike creature and wisp of a nine-year-old could have nothing to do with Sir Brangwyn's disappearance.

When it was clear that Sir Brangwyn was gone for good, all his lands—the castle, the village, and the deep, dark woods—passed to his son. The younger Sir Brangwyn was far gentler than his father. As his first act as lord of the castle, he set all its prisoners free. As his second, he opened its stores and held a great feast for the village.

Rhiannon and her parents were happy to attend. They even brought truffles.

THE DWARF

You probably know of Arthur Pendragon, the legendary British king who pulled the shining sword Excalibur from a stone to take his place as ruler of Camelot. Legends tell of his reign as the head of the Knights of the Round Table, of his friendship with the wizard Merlin, and of the battles he fought to defend his kingdom against invaders. They also tell of a sea voyage he took early in his reign when, shipwrecked on an island, he met a very unusual trio.

Arthur's ship was sailing in the North Sea, off the coast of Northumbria (in what is now southern Scotland), when a vicious storm blew in from the arctic. Gale winds tore at the ship's single mast and clawed at the riggings. They tossed the ship and spurred the sea into giant waves that crashed over its decks and threatened to drag it under. They had no choice but to bring down the sail to keep it from being destroyed.

It quickly became clear that the rowers were helpless, too, in the face of the waves, and so the crew could only sit by as the storm blew them off course and pray they would make it through alive. They drifted that way, soaked to the bone and helpless, for hours. Until, with a lurch that threw them to the decks, the ship finally crashed ashore on the rocky beach of an island.

When the sea was calmer, and the lashing rains had faded, Arthur climbed down to the beach. He looked over his ship to assess the damage. It had taken a beating, but it was sound. It would take days to repair the rigging and push it back to sea, so he gave orders to his crew, then turned his attention to the island they had come to. This was a land entirely unknown to him and his crew. It didn't appear on any maps and had never been mentioned in any of the stories told by seafarers. He resolved to explore it while his crew repaired the boat.

The wide pebble beach led up to a piney forest. Where it touched the shore, the trees were stunted and gnarled, twisted by the constant wind that came off the sea. Beyond, the trees grew larger and closer together. Arthur could only see a few feet into the woods before shapes were lost in the shadow. Still, he pushed past the outer ring of trees and into the woods beyond. When he had been walking for quite a while, he came upon a clearing. At its center, surrounded by a little lawn of grass and wildflowers, was a gray stone tower, at least twenty feet tall. Arthur circled the tower twice, looking for a door or window, but he found nothing that could be used as an entrance. It did have four windows, one on each side, but they were about fifteen feet up the bare walls and looked out over the tops of the trees.

Arthur had almost given up when he thought he heard a noise coming from one of the windows.

"Hello!" he called. "Is someone there?"

His call was met with silence. So he tried again. "Hello?"

After a moment, a head poked out of the window. The face was covered in lines and folds that told of long years spent in the sun. It was ringed by wispy strands of white hair, and it was not overly polite.

"Who are you?" the man in the tower said gruffly.

"I am Arthur Pendragon," Arthur replied, "king of Camelot. My ship was stranded here in the storm. Tell me—what is this island? And who are *you*?"

The man in the tower sighed. "What this island is, I do not know. I, too, have been stranded here for many, many years. But who I am I will gladly tell you."

Then, leaning out his window high in the tower, he told King Arthur this story:

"I come from Northumbria, where I did not have an easy life. I know you cannot see me properly while I am high up in this tower, so I'll tell you that I'm a dwarf. In these dark and superstitious times, many look upon people who are different with suspicion. In my homeland, I had to work twice as hard as others to earn my keep and promise twice as much to my neighbors to keep the peace.

"But I was resourceful enough, and I managed to scrape by. When I was still young, I met a woman who loved me unconditionally, and I loved her endlessly. We were happy together, so we were luckier than most.

"We had not been married long before we were expecting a baby, and we were thrilled at the prospect of a child. But before the baby was born, famine struck the region. Crops began to wilt and many ran out of food. The king went looking for a scapegoat, and he didn't need to look any further than me. I was accused of witchcraft—of putting a curse on the land around me—and banished from the kingdom.

"My wife and I were bound in rope and led to the shore, where a small wooden boat awaited us. We huddled together on the hard wood planks of the hull as the boat was pushed into the steely gray of the North Sea. A team of grim-faced rowers steered the boat through the chop and icy spray for hours, until at last we arrived at this island.

"In the fog and gloom, it was a forbidding place. It was clear from the desolation on the beach that no humans lived here. It was a cold afternoon, but nowhere was there a sign of a fire—the telltale chimney smoke of a house or a village. Clouds were gathering in the distance, a sure sign that a storm would arrive soon.

"The rowers removed the ropes that bound us. They scarcely gave me time to help my wife to shore before they pulled hard on their oars and disappeared into the fog.

"That night, my wife went into labor on the rocky beach. The baby was early, and there was certainly no midwife on the island. I did my best, but not long after the baby—a boy—was born, my wife died.

"I was heartbroken and marooned on this deserted island, but I wasn't alone. There was nothing I could do to bring back my wife, but I knew that I would have to find shelter in order to save our child. I swaddled the infant in my wife's cloak and carried him into the woods.

"Lightning flashed, and the first drops of rain began to fall as I stumbled into the trees, tripping on their gnarled roots in the dark. The trees near the shore were too scrubby to provide much shelter, so I moved farther and farther inland. Before long, I came across a giant pine tree. I inspected it, hoping for a low branch that would provide us some shelter, or a furrow in the trunk that we could huddle against for protection. I was rewarded beyond my wildest dreams—feeling around the trunk I found an opening that led into a hollow inside it. It was a large chamber, warm and dry, and certainly big enough for me to climb inside with my little bundle.

"I scrambled inside and settled down, relieved to at least have found safety. The storm had reached the island, and rain was coming down in sheets. Flashes of lightning lit the inside of the tree.

"That was when I realized that my son and I were not alone.

"Three long-legged fawns lolled sleepily nearby. Each had the tawny fur, soft noses, and deep brown eyes of a deer fawn, but on their foreheads they each had a little button of bone—the beginnings of a single horn. Whatever they were, they were very young and content to drowse together in a heap, their body heat keeping each other warm.

"They clearly didn't pose a danger to us, so my baby and I curled together with them in the hollow. I'd had a very long and devastating day, and despite myself, I quickly fell asleep.

"Hours later, I was awakened by the sound of a horse snorting and roaring in rage. Still bleary with sleep, I looked around. Sunlight was streaming around the edges of the entrance to the tree hollow, but most of the doorway was filled with the bulk of a massive animal. As it lunged toward me, leaving the doorway open, I saw my chance. I darted for the exit and threw myself out into the forest.

"It was only once I was out in the cold morning light, my heart pounding in my chest, that everything that had happened the day

before came flooding back to me. I realized in a rush of horror that I had left my own baby in the tree hollow, snuggled tight with the fawns. Deeply ashamed of my own cowardice, and devastated that I had lost the one precious thing I had left, I hid in the woods and wept.

"It was only hours later, when I had managed to pull myself together, that I crept back to the hollow tree. I peeked inside and realized my son was still alive.

"Inside the cozy tree hollow, a unicorn was curled up. She was large and white, as big as a horse with a deadly horn on her forehead. Her three tiny foals were curled next to her, nursing, and there alongside them was my son.

"I knew that the unicorn could take better care of my son than I could. After all, she could feed the baby, and I had no way to do that. And she could certainly protect him from other animals. But I could not bring myself to leave the boy behind, so I waited beside the tree until the unicorn left, then crawled in to check on him. I changed and washed him, then covered him in kisses and set him back among the fawns.

"I continued to do this for several days, until one day the unicorn came back and caught me in the act. But this time, she didn't lunge at me. Instead, she whickered agreeably and came slowly into the hollow. I stayed where I was as she settled into her spot and fed the babies, and I slowly realized that the unicorn had accepted us as part of her family.

"The unicorn and I lived together in the tree hollow with our babies for quite some time. She helped me hunt for food, and my son grew so quickly from drinking unicorn milk that he soon reached the size of a giant. In fact, before long, all the young were

too large for our little home. The foals grew up and set out on their own, but human babies need their parents for much longer than unicorn foals do. The unicorn, my son, and I stayed together. And we stayed together even after my son was full-grown. Like the unicorn, he was so big and strong that he didn't need to fear the other creatures on the island, but I needed protection.

"When he was old enough, my son built me this tower of stone. Although it may seem massive to you, it only came to his shoulder, and was only the work of a few days for him to build. When I want to enter the tower, my son lifts me to the top, where a staircase leads down to a safe and cozy room.

"Sometimes, the unicorn, my son, and I still hunt together. But as I grow older, I am often content to stay in my tower and watch the sea. On the clearest of days, I can sometimes see a faint shimmer on the horizon—a thin line of land a hundred miles away across the wide sea. On those days, I remember my years in Northumbria, and the sweet months I spent there with my wife.

"Then I think of this wild island, the magnificent unicorn who is my constant companion, and my strong, healthy son, and I realize that I am finally home."

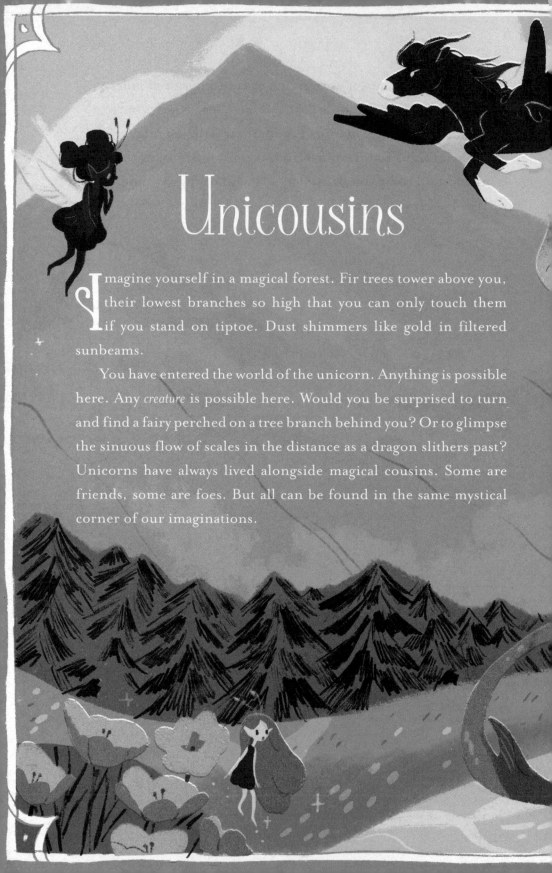

Unicousins

Imagine yourself in a magical forest. Fir trees tower above you, their lowest branches so high that you can only touch them if you stand on tiptoe. Dust shimmers like gold in filtered sunbeams.

You have entered the world of the unicorn. Anything is possible here. Any *creature* is possible here. Would you be surprised to turn and find a fairy perched on a tree branch behind you? Or to glimpse the sinuous flow of scales in the distance as a dragon slithers past? Unicorns have always lived alongside magical cousins. Some are friends, some are foes. But all can be found in the same mystical corner of our imaginations.

PEGASUS

It's hard to imagine that anything could be as beautiful as a unicorn. With their flowing manes and tails, perfectly spiraling horns, and incredible swiftness, unicorns are an unbeatable combination of horse and magic. Nothing can even come close.

Except perhaps Pegasus.

While unicorns first appeared in the records of ancient Greek naturalists, who were trying to record the real animals of the world, Pegasus is a creature of Greek mythology, stories full of adventure and magic. He's a steed fit for battle between men and monsters, a horse even swifter than a unicorn—so swift, in fact, that he can fly. And unlike unicorns, which appeared all over the world, there is only one Pegasus.

The story of Pegasus isn't exactly pretty. In fact, it's kind of bloody. It begins with three deadly sisters called the Gorgons, terrible winged monsters covered in golden scales. Instead of flowing hair, each had a nest of hissing, writhing snakes on her head. Anyone who looked directly at a Gorgon was instantly turned to stone.

One night, the hero Perseus snuck into the Gorgons' lair. He had foolishly promised the head of one of the Gorgons, Medusa, to his soon-to-be stepfather. Using the reflection in his golden shield, Perseus was able to cut off Medusa's head without looking directly at her.

It was a great end to Perseus's adventure, but it was also the beginning of a completely new story: A magnificent winged horse named Pegasus sprang from the blood of the dead Gorgon.

After his strange birth, Pegasus ran free. He made a home near Mount Helicon, where he created a spring by striking the ground with one of his powerful hooves. It was at that spring that he was captured by another mortal hero, Bellerophon. Carrying a golden bridle that had been given to him by the goddess Athena, Bellerophon crept up on Pegasus as the stallion was drinking from the spring. Pegasus was so charmed by the divine bridle that he allowed Bellerophon to slip it over his head and climb onto his back.

Together, Pegasus and Bellerophon were unstoppable. According to an ancient Greek poet, Pegasus was "a winged steed, unwearying of flight, sweeping through the air, swift as a gale of wind." They defeated the chimera, a deadly, fire-breathing monster with a lion's head, a goat's body, and a serpent's tail; and survived battle against the Solymi and the Amazons, two ferocious tribes of warriors.

Unfortunately, Bellerophon got a little too big for his britches. He decided that he deserved to fly to Mount Olympus and take a place among the gods. Pegasus, however, was much wiser than his master and knew that the gods would be insulted by a mere mortal trying to join them. He bucked Bellerophon off his back and flew on to Olympus alone.

There, the immortal Pegasus did what Bellerophon could never have done and took a place among the gods. He became a part of the stable at Mount Olympus, the most magnificent horse in the herd. Pegasus was so beloved and trusted by the gods that he was given an incredibly important job: carrying Zeus's thunderbolts into battle.

Today, many of Pegasus's deeds have been forgotten. In fact, you'll often hear people refer to "a pegasus" or many "pegasi," as though there could have been more than one. But there was only ever one Pegasus, a magnificent, swift stallion with wings strong enough to carry the gods.

Immortalized in the Stars

At the end of his story, Pegasus flew to the heavens to join the gods on Mount Olympus, but he wasn't entirely lost to us here on earth. In fact, you can still see him in the heavens—as a constellation.

The constellation Pegasus has been included in star charts since at least the second century CE. You can spot it in the northern sky by looking for the distinct square that forms Pegasus's body. Once you've found him, you don't have far to go to find the constellation Perseus, which commemorates the hero whose gory adventure brought Pegasus to life.

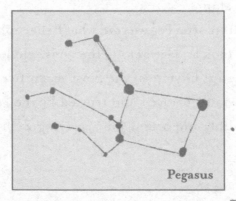

Pegasus

HIPPOCAMPI

Pegasus may have dominated the land and sky, but there was one part of the world where he was powerless: the sea. And that was really a problem, because the Greek god Poseidon, lord of the sea, spent a lot of his time there.

In the religion of ancient Greece, people worshipped many gods and goddesses (called a pantheon). Responsibility for the natural world was divided among them. People who needed help would pray to the specific gods who could help them with their problems. Worried about the weather? Pray to Zeus, lord of the sky. Heading out on a sea voyage? Make a sacrifice to Poseidon, ruler of the seas. Apollo was in charge of the sun, Athena was the goddess of wisdom, Demeter of the harvest—and on and on.

Along with lesser deities, there were twelve major gods who lived on Mount Olympus, each representing a different aspect of the world. But while there were a lot of gods, there was also a lot of world to cover, so each of the gods was associated with many, many parts of life.

Along with his job as lord of the sea, Poseidon was also the father of horses. According to the myth, Poseidon fell in love with Demeter, goddess of the harvest. Unfortunately for him, she didn't feel the same way. Rather than reject Poseidon outright, Demeter gave him an impossible challenge: She asked him to create the most beautiful animal in the world.

Hippocampus comes from two Greek words: *hippo*, which means "horse," and *campus*, which means "sea monster." The plural of *hippocampus* is *hippocampi*.

The name hippocampus was also given to a part of the human brain that is shaped like a seahorse, and to a tiny moon—just twenty-two miles across—that orbits the planet Neptune.

It was definitely a difficult challenge—Poseidon created a lot of critters that were less than perfect before he hit upon the final animal—but it was far from impossible. Eventually, he came up with the horse.

The task had taken him so long that he was not in love with Demeter anymore by the time it was finished, but it was worth it all the same. In trying to woo Demeter, he had given himself—and the world—an animal that was both beautiful and useful.

Magnificent though they were, Poseidon didn't stick to plain old garden-variety horses. He was also the father of Pegasus. And to keep him company under the sea, he came up with the Hippocampus.

Hippocampi were magnificent creatures of the sea. From the waist up, they resembled land-bound horses, with arching necks, long legs, and thundering hooves. From the waist down, Hippocampi had the strong, flexible bodies of fish, with shimmering, colorful scales and powerful tails to propel them through the water.

Just as people on land relied on horses to get around in ancient Greece, naiads—or sea nymphs—counted on hippocampi for travel in rivers and streams. Poseidon himself traveled in a chariot drawn by hippocampi.

But hippocampi weren't found only in Greek mythology. Images of winged hippocampi appear on gold coins minted in Tyre, which is now Lebanon, around 400 BCE, and carvings of winged hippocampi were common in Etruscan tombs (a culture found in what is now Italy), where they appear to be guarding the afterlife. Hippocampi were also steeds to the Roman god of the sea, Neptune.

Many of the people living in these ancient cultures on the Mediterranean Sea believed that the fish that we now call seahorses were babies that would grow up into powerful hippocampi. Perhaps in honor of that legend, modern scientists classify seahorses in the genus *hippocampus*, which includes seahorses, sea dragons, and pipe fish.

WINGED UNICORNS

What's better than a unicorn or a flying horse? How about a unicorn that *is* a flying horse?

It's not clear exactly when these two creatures came together into one magnificent mythological beast. The earliest known winged unicorns were depicted in artwork from the Assyrian Empire (in what is now Iraq) more than two thousand years ago. But the Assyrian unicorn was more of an ox than a horse. And in Europe, it was an entirely different story. For millennia, the European unicorn and Pegasus kept to their separate corners.

Ready for Battle

Thousands of years after it was first told, the powerful Pegasus story is still winning people over. Pegasus and Bellerophon's skill in fighting from the sky made them powerful symbols for fighter pilots during World War II. Members of the British Airborne units wore patches that depicted the mythical hero, spear raised for battle, on Pegasus's back. But in some depictions, Pegasus sports a feature that he didn't have in the Greek myths: a unicorn horn.

The wild, pure unicorn of medieval tapestries and coats of arms was a part of Christian lore. Pegasus, the rugged steed, belonged to Greek mythology. And the two never seemed to meet. But that all changed sometime in the twentieth century, when references to flying unicorns became common.

Then came the 1980s, when unicornimania took over. Unicorns and rainbows became popular motifs on everything from posters and T-shirts to lunch boxes and tattoos. Unicorns popped up in children's books and public murals. And perhaps more importantly, they began to appear in cartoons.

In 1984, toy company Hasbro introduced a line of plastic horses they called My Little Pony, which included both unicorns and winged horses. They would soon produce television specials and movies based on the wildly popular toys. In the world of classic My Little Pony, unicorns and flying horses remained separate. But with unicorns everywhere, it was only a matter of time before some of them sprouted wings.

When they did, it created a conundrum: What do you call a winged unicorn? When novelist Piers Anthony included one in his 1984 book *Bearing an Hourglass*, he called it an alicorn, sparking years of debate. Unicorn purists know that *alicorn* is the name for a unicorn's horn, and argue that using it to describe a winged unicorn can only cause confusion. Still, the name has stuck around. In 2010, when the rebooted My Little Pony TV show *My Little Pony: Friendship Is Magic* included flying unicorns, they were called alicorns. Some people prefer "pegacorn." Whatever you call them, it's clear that winged unicorns are here to stay.

Winged unicorns combine the magic and wildness of unicorns with the speed and aerial acrobatics of Pegasus. They're an elusive creature that promises adventure—like a unicorn, they are difficult to find and even more difficult to catch. But for the lucky few who can find a way to tame one, they promise a ride through the clouds.

DRAGONS

If unicorns represent virtue and innocence, European dragons are the dark and dangerous flipside of the same magical coin. The dragon is a massive lizard that represents evil in medieval tales. But its story, although far darker and more sinister, begins in much the same way as the unicorn's.

Like unicorns, dragons first appeared in ancient Roman texts by Pliny the Elder and Aelian, then made their way into medieval bestiaries. But while unicorns were often associated with Jesus in medieval tales, dragons were stand-ins for the devil. They varied a lot in early stories, sometimes appearing without legs, or with several extras—one version had eight! But gradually the dragon morphed into a recognizable monster. A dragon's tightly meshing scales could be almost any color, its armored body one of many shapes. But if it's a European dragon, it probably has one or more of these traits:

◊ **IT IS LARGE,** so large that it can destroy a band of noble knights with a single sweep of its enormous tail. Even the earliest bestiaries emphasized the dragon's formidable size. To make the point, stories often pitted the dragon against an elephant. Using its long, muscular tail, the dragon would strangle or drown the elephant. Later, dragons became known for swooping out of the sky and striking their victims down with their tails.

◊ **IT HAS THICK LEGS,** like tree trunks. Of course, moving around with a body that large requires some hefty support. Most dragons have four legs, but a smaller category of dragons, known as wyverns, are two-legged. Both varieties make their homes underground, in burrows or caves, which means they need diamond-sharp claws for digging.

◊ **IT CAN FLY.** Not every dragon can go airborne, but most can—on leathery wings so massive that they block out the sun when the dragon wheels overhead. Although it's most common to find dragons with one enormous set of two, occasionally they need four wings to keep aloft.

◊ **IT BREATHES FIRE.** Medieval dragons often killed their victims with their poisonous breath, but more often than not modern dragons scorch would-be slayers with flames.

◊ **IT COVETS GOLD.** Although the idea of dragons guarding a horde has been around for centuries, it probably owes much of its popularity to J. R. R. Tolkien, who depicted the dragon Smaug atop a mountain of treasure in his 1937 novel *The Hobbit*. Dragons can often be found lying on a pile of treasure and bones. They gather their gold over centuries, scraping together a heap of wealth and guarding it jealously. The bones pile up when adventurers arrive hoping to slay the dragon and take the treasure for themselves. They rarely succeed and instead provide a tasty snack for the dragon, as well as armor and swords to add to the dragon's wealth.

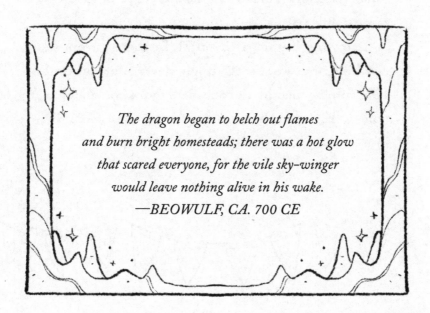

The dragon began to belch out flames
and burn bright homesteads; there was a hot glow
that scared everyone, for the vile sky-winger
would leave nothing alive in his wake.
—BEOWULF, CA. 700 CE

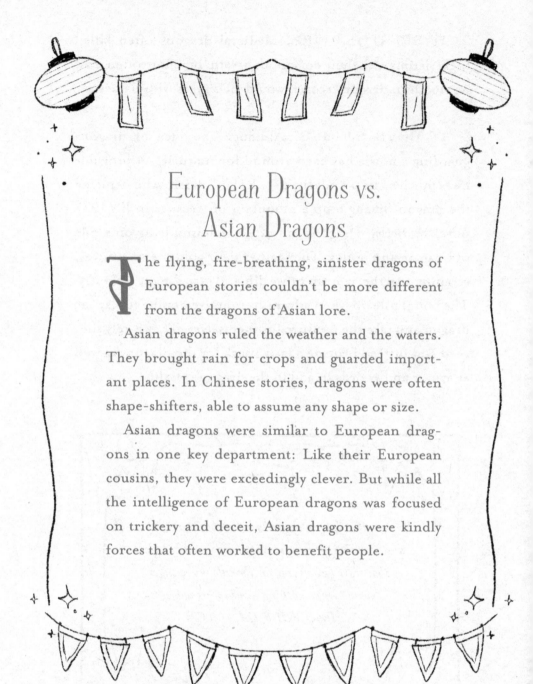

European Dragons vs. Asian Dragons

The flying, fire-breathing, sinister dragons of European stories couldn't be more different from the dragons of Asian lore.

Asian dragons ruled the weather and the waters. They brought rain for crops and guarded important places. In Chinese stories, dragons were often shape-shifters, able to assume any shape or size.

Asian dragons were similar to European dragons in one key department: Like their European cousins, they were exceedingly clever. But while all the intelligence of European dragons was focused on trickery and deceit, Asian dragons were kindly forces that often worked to benefit people.

MERMAIDS

Imagine being a sailor on a ship thousands of years ago. All around you, as far as you can see, there is nothing but sky and sea. You haven't seen a blip of land in weeks, and you don't know if you ever will again. The seascape is barren, but it isn't empty. Beneath the waves, danger lurks. You have heard stories of the kraken, a massive, tentacled beast that can pull an entire ship underwater, and killer storms that will blow it to pieces. Along with those disasters, you also fear mermaids.

The mermaid is another fantastical creature that made its way from the bestiaries to every corner of the medieval world. Carved into the prows of sailing ships and featured in stories told below decks, sea maidens were carried far and wide. Stories of mermaids were told in Africa and Asia, Europe and the Americas. But no matter where the tale came from, the mermaids themselves looked pretty much the same: They were usually beautiful, with long flowing hair and perfectly formed human bodies from the waist up. From the waist down, they had the tails and fins of fish.

Although they may have looked the same, mermaids in different traditions had very different personalities. In some stories, mermaids were evil temptresses who lured sailors to their doom, pulling them into the depths or tempting them to crash their ships onto the rocks. Unsurprisingly, many sailors considered mermaids a curse to be avoided on their journeys.

But in other tales, mermaids were silly and vain—and mostly harmless. (In medieval paintings, they are often seen holding a mirror and a comb, two symbols of vanity.) In this tradition, the mermaids longed to have a human soul, and the only way to get one was to marry a man. Romantic tales of mermaids finding human husbands had been around for centuries before Hans Christian Andersen wrote the most famous version, "The Little Mermaid," in 1837.

How did mermaids develop such different personalities? The confusion probably came from storytellers mixing up mermaids and sirens, another human/animal combination. In Greek myths, the sirens were a mixture of women and birds, usually depicted as having bird bodies and human heads. A famous Greek epic, the *Odyssey*, written by Homer in the eighth century BCE, featured sirens who sang so sweetly that sailors passing by the craggy rocks where the sirens sat would leap into the water and swim to their deaths. Over time, the sirens began to change shape. As stories of mermaids spread, the sirens gained decidedly fish-shaped tails. During the Middle Ages, sirens remained evil, dangerous creatures and mermaids beautiful, vain creatures, but they appeared in the same bestiaries, and often they were both shown as half woman, half fish. Is it any wonder that some people got confused?

When sailors crossed the Atlantic Ocean during the Age of Exploration, they kept their eyes peeled for sea monsters of all kinds. But the mermaids' iffy reputation didn't seem to bother Christopher Columbus, who claimed to have spotted three off the Dominican coast in 1493. He wasn't worried about bad luck, but he was disappointed in their appearance, writing that they were "not as pretty as they are depicted, for somehow in the face they look like men."

Many historians agree that Columbus really saw manatees, not mermaids. If you want to try to find your own mermaid, though, head for rocky spots in bays and harbors. Mermaids are creatures of the open water, but let's be honest—it's hard to spot a single mermaid in the vast sea. When men have encountered mermaids, they have often caught them sunning themselves in places where rocks jut from the sea. If you encounter a mermaid, it will most likely be where the shore meets the ocean.

FAIRIES

Do you think of fairies as delightful magical creatures that flit around on butterfly wings spreading magical fairy dust wherever they go? Or maybe as something a little larger, like the fairy godmother in "Cinderella," who appears in a time of need and grants wishes that save the day? If so, you might want to think again.

That's the modern idea of a fairy, but fairy stories have been around for a very, very long time. And the fairies themselves have taken on very different forms.

In some stories they are tall and thin, skeletal creatures that look a lot like humans. In others they are short and trollish. In still others, they are the mesmerizing tiny creatures with wings that you often see today.

It's hard to know which is the "true" fairy, but no matter what form they take, one thing is certain: Fairies are not to be trusted. They may look like lovely little humans—just smaller and with adorable wings—but they are something entirely different. They are creatures of dark, mysterious magic who live in a world entirely separate from ours. They don't worry much about human life. If you stumble into their path, they may take notice. But that is not necessarily a good thing.

In old stories, fairies were often portrayed as wicked creatures. A weary traveler making his way through the dense, dark forest at night might spot a fairy light in the distance. Dancing playfully along until the traveler followed, it would lead him to a treacherous bog—then disappear. More than one unfortunate hero was invited to visit the fairies, only to find that when he returned to the human realm, hundreds of years had passed. And fairies were implicated in many a legendary kidnapping—of both adults and children.

The most unsettling stories of fairies featured changelings. Fairies would sneak into the windows of homes where there was a new baby and steal the infant from its crib. Sometimes, they would leave behind a wooden doll to replace the baby. But more often, the story goes, they would leave a changeling—a fairy baby that might have been bewitched to make it look like the stolen infant. Medieval parents believed that babies were vulnerable to fairies until they were baptized, and would watch over them closely.

Other stories painted the fairies as merely mischievous. These fairies would creep into your room at night and tie your hair into knots. Or they may hide an important item, like your keys or your homework. Whether the fairy mischief was harmless or deadly, fairies loved to mess with humans.

Fortunately, there were ways to discourage fairies from bothering you. Fairies are said to be afraid of iron, so keeping metal objects around will repel them. A four-leaf clover is also a powerful anti-fairy charm. If you can't find one, try wearing your clothes inside out.

But the best defense against fairy mischief is to stay out of the fairies' way. Avoid clearings where they meet at night, do not pitch your camp along a fairy highway, and if you meet one, be polite—but get away as quickly as you can.

It is true that fairies have powerful magic, and if they're feeling inclined they can be extremely helpful. But even their good deeds can turn out to be pranks. More than one fairy-tale character accepted a gift of fairy gold, only to find it was a worthless pile of stones once the fairies were far away.

If you're still thinking of searching for fairies, or building a fairy house in the hope that they will come to you, good luck. They are notoriously difficult to find. Fairies live underground and usually prefer to stay hidden. They can deploy glamour, a magical trick to disguise themselves—and some have even been reported to shape-shift, changing into other animals to escape detection. In fact, of all the magical creatures, fairies—with their magical means to confuse you—might be the most elusive. And that's a good thing. Really.

Wee Folk

You've heard of fairies and elves, but what about brownies, pixies, or sprites? Fairy tales are full of tiny, magical creatures that may help out their human neighbors or cause them trouble. Although they each have unique characteristics—brownies, for example, live in human houses and sneak out to do housework at night, while pixies are woodland creatures—they are more alike than they are different.

All look like very small humans and have extraordinary magical powers. They all share a dark side. And many of the same stories are told about them. Both elves and fairies are known to steal babies, and both fairies and pixies have been known to lead travelers astray in the woods. In the end, the differences are mostly the result of where they came from. Cultures all over the world have stories of wee folk, and each one, drawing on local languages and traditions, gave them different names.

Unicorns Today

Unicorn history is all well and good. But let's face it: Modern unicorns can be a lot more appealing. You may be tempted to try to track one down in the wild. You wouldn't be the first. But before you head out, there's a lot you need to know.

Unicorns have changed a lot—both in appearance and personality—since the days of the early Greek and Roman naturalists. Arm yourself with the facts about unicorn behavior before you find yourself face-to-face with the most wild and beautiful legendary creature.

ANATOMY

Unicorns may look like horses with horns, but their magical properties make them quite different. Here are some of the unique features that distinguish them from their non-magical cousins.

Horn

Tail

Mane

Muzzle

Heart

Hooves

◊ The MUZZLE is softer and more velvety than that of any other animal in the real or mythical world.

◊ The HORN is the source of the unicorn's power, and a useful magical tool in its own right. It has the power to heal and can purify any water source.

◊ As creatures that can move between the human world and magical realms, unicorns can see both, and cannot be deceived by magical means.

◊ It is believed that unicorns can understand all human languages, although further testing is needed to confirm this.

◊ Unlike horse hooves, unicorn HOOVES cannot be trimmed or punctured by nails to attach shoes. Fortunately, they don't need to be—unicorn magic keeps them pristine.

◊ Perhaps surprisingly, unicorns are of an average height for a horse, between 15 and 16 hands (5 feet and 5 feet 4 inches) tall at the withers.

◊ Many unicorns today still have feathered fetlocks as they did in the Middle Ages.

◊ A unicorn's HEART is pure and strong and doesn't weaken with age. To date, no unicorn is known to have died of old age, or even to have shown any signs of slowing down with age.

◊ Swifter than all animals in the human realm, unicorns can also outrun motorcycles, cars, and trucks. Experiments have not yet been conducted with aircraft.

◊ The hair of the MANE and TAIL cannot be cut. But should you find some, caught on a thistle or drifting in the wind, it can be used to form a powerful charm. Wind the hair around your wrist and another around the wrist of a friend or loved one to create an unbreakable bond.

HABITAT

Have you ever wondered why unicorns are so hard to find? The answer lies in their ability to slip back and forth between the magical and human worlds.

When they're not galloping through meadows and visiting cool mountain springs, unicorns hide in the magical realm. It's difficult to say what that world is like—no one outside of legend has been there and returned—but you can catch glimmers of it through fairy tales and legends.

Medieval Europeans referred to this realm as Faerie, the land where the fae, or fairy people, lived. Faerie is a parallel world—a place that is never far away but always hidden from view. Time passes differently there. Visitors have spent a day in Faerie, only to return to the human world and find that many years—sometimes even hundreds!—have passed. Shocking as that might be, those were the lucky ones. Most human visitors to Faerie never return. But magical creatures can enter and leave Faerie through secret doors.

Doorways to Faerie are often found on fairy mounds or in tree trunks, or between two fairy trees. Since unicorns' size makes them unlikely to travel through the portals in trunks and mounds, that means their trips to the human world most frequently land them in forests where two fairy trees might grow close together.

While traditional fairy tales named hawthorn and ash trees as types most likely to be used as fairy doorways, it's possible for other species to host portals as well. What's more important than the species of tree is its age. Magical doorways are ancient things, established centuries ago. That means that the only remaining portals can be found in old-growth forests, places where trees have grown uncut for hundreds of years.

Shrinking World

These days, old-growth forests are few and far between. And the forests that remain are under constant threat from logging and land development. That means that unicorn habitat in the human world is in danger of vanishing entirely. But as long as the old-growth forests remain, they'll offer a chance to see a unicorn.

How can you tell one forest from another? It takes a scientist to determine whether a forest is young or old, but there are some signs you might be able to identify.

Look for very large trees. Old-growth trees have been growing for centuries and can have trunks that are as large as sixty feet in diameter. The canopy in an old-growth forest towers high overhead. The forest floor is uneven, covered in pits and mounds left when ancient trees fell over and decayed, and it is thick with humus, soft soil left behind when fallen leaves and branches dissolve into the ground. Thick moss grows everywhere. The forest smells of earth and ferns and, in cold climates, the Christmassy scent of pine.

Unicorns are hardy creatures and will visit forests in any climate. They rest in the shade in southern forests and gallop through the snows up north. They don't need to eat when they're in our world, but they are known to be attracted to natural springs. Look for them in places where water burbles from the ground into quiet pools.

Unicorn Habitat Checklist

Look for these signs of magic to determine whether your forest might be a good place for a unicorn sighting:

◊ **LARGE OLD TREES** If you can reach your arms around a tree, it is unlikely to hide a doorway to Faerie.

◊ **FAIRY RINGS** Mushroom circles and unusually perfect circles of grass in the woods are known to be places where fairies meet. A doorway to the magical realm cannot be far away.

◊ **NATURAL SPRINGS** Unicorns generally avoid food in the human realm but cannot resist a visit to a natural spring.

◊ **GLIMMERS OF LIGHT** A unicorn doorway will be found between two trees of the same type. It is difficult to see with the naked eye, but some talented spotters might recognize a difference in the light between the trunks.

◊ **UNUSUAL STILLNESS** In warm weather, forests are filled with the sounds of animals: songbirds calling, mosquitoes buzzing, woodpeckers drumming. But magical doorways are surrounded by pockets of stillness, where those sounds fall away. Listen carefully as you move through the woods and take note of locations where the forest is suddenly silent.

TRACKING

Finding a magical forest is only the first of many steps you'll have to take before you'll see an actual unicorn. After all, even the most remote unicorn forests are visited by humans these days. Yet few, if any, of those visitors will actually see a unicorn. Magical creatures go to great pains to stay out of sight of mortals—you won't simply stumble upon one on your daily walk. If you want to observe a unicorn in the wild, you'll need stealth and solid tracking skills.

Your best bet for a unicorn encounter is to use your knowledge of unicorn behavior to find a place in the woods that a unicorn is likely to visit. Once you've identified a unicorn-friendly place in the woods, you can establish a hide—a concealed place where you can wait until the unicorn appears.

There are two natural places to wait for a unicorn: a fairy door or an enchanted spring. Both are likely to be used by any unicorn in a magical forest. A spring is more likely to yield results than a doorway, but since both are difficult to locate, it is best to take advantage of whatever you can find.

UNICORN DOORS

Since there are so few Faerie portals that are large enough for a horse-sized beast, an open door is often used by many unicorns. That makes them a prime location to hide and wait for a unicorn to come to you. But they can make for tricky unicorn spotting, since any unicorn near a door will leap through it at the first sign of any trouble. The doorways can also be difficult to locate in the first place.

Look for two large old trees close together. The natural V

formed by a two-trunked tree is also a possibility.* A good spot-ter may be able to see the doorway between them, but don't be surprised if you can't. While many unicorn spotters can see a dif-ference in the light between the trunks of a doorway, the effect is extremely subtle.

Humans cannot see through the portals to the world of Faerie—if you are standing right in front of a unicorn door, you will simply see more forest on the other side. But the doors are constantly open-ing and closing, allowing small or even invisible magical creatures through. When the door opens, light from the other world escapes. Since time in Faerie is out of sync with our world, the light streaming through will be subtly different than the light on our side. This is most conspicuous when it is night in Faerie. Then the doorway will cast a shadow for which there is no apparent explanation. But more subtle differences in light can still be visible. You may be walking through the woods at midday and notice the rosy glow of sunrise or sunset coming through the portal. Or the warm glow of summer may cut through the cold blue light of a winter day.

NATURAL SPRINGS

Enchanted springs are much easier to locate. While it's difficult to tell an enchanted spring from any other natural spring, it's a fair bet that any spring in a unicorn forest is enchanted. That's because the spring's magic comes from the unicorn itself. Uni-corns are drawn to them, and dip their horns into the water as they drink, purifying and enchanting the water. Because springs are so

---

* Note that it is not necessary for a unicorn door to appear near the ground. Unicorns are extremely agile and can jump through a door as high as ten feet up. Winged unicorns, of course, can fly through doors that are high in the trees, and even prefer them, but require a wider door to accommodate their massive wings.

attractive to unicorns, you will have a greater chance to find a unicorn there than you would at a unicorn door.

Keep in mind, though, that unicorns do not appreciate all sources of water equally. Puddles, ponds, streams, and lakes are unlikely to attract them. To identify a natural spring, look for a place where water is coming up from the ground. Natural spring water makes its way to the surface from an aquifer, a pocket of water stored deep underground in the rock. It usually follows underground fissures, seams in the rock that channel the water to the surface, which means that many natural springs come out of the ground in rocky places. Today, many known natural springs have been tapped by humans—the water comes from a pipe that has been built into the spring to make the water easier to collect. These natural springs will appear on maps, which makes them much easier to locate.

It is possible for an underground water source to originate from surface water. Rainwater and other runoff travels underground and emerges elsewhere. If you find a source of water coming from the ground and are unsure whether it is runoff or a spring, check its temperature. The temperature of the spring water will be consistent no matter what the weather. Generally, it is quite cold even on the hottest days, although it's possible for a natural spring to be heated by volcanic activity. In that case, it will remain consistently warm throughout the spring, summer, fall, and winter.

Natural springs also run consistently throughout the year, even in the driest weather. Other sources of water will be stronger in the spring and may dry to a trickle in the heat of summer.

UNICORN SIGN

If you can't find an obvious spring or doorway, you can attempt to locate one by tracking unicorn sign. Despite their large size, unicorns don't make much noise as they move through the woods. But like any animal, they create *sign*—changes to the forest that are left by their passage. A good tracker will recognize unicorn sign and can follow the animal's trail back to its doorway or water source.

Tracking is always easier after a light snow when a thin layer of white powder makes it particularly easy to spot animal tracks, but it's possible to find good tracks at any time of the year.

Look for places where the ground is particularly soft. Sand is a good surface, as is wet dirt. (If mud is too wet, though, tracks become sloppy.) If a unicorn has passed that way recently, it is likely to have left one or more hoofprints. Be careful not to confuse horse hoofprints for unicorn tracks, though.

Like a horse, unicorns leave a round hoofprint. But most horses wear shoes, which leave a familiar U-shaped

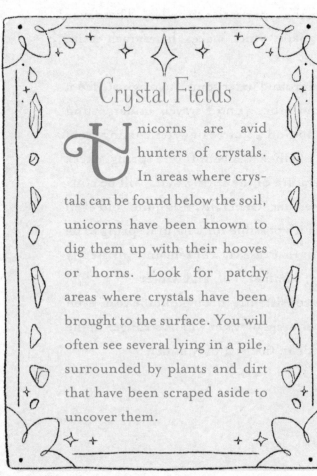

Crystal Fields

Unicorns are avid hunters of crystals. In areas where crystals can be found below the soil, unicorns have been known to dig them up with their hooves or horns. Look for patchy areas where crystals have been brought to the surface. You will often see several lying in a pile, surrounded by plants and dirt that have been scraped aside to uncover them.

print. Unicorn prints resemble the print of an unshod horse and look a bit like a circle with a triangle cutting into it. They range from about four inches to six inches across. And while horse hooves are

slightly elongated—they are longer from front to back than from side to side—unicorn hooves are perfectly round. Some trackers insist that a unicorn's print shimmers slightly in direct sunlight and may even glow at night, but this is controversial.

If you are fortunate enough to come across a hoofprint, use it as your starting point. Look for more hoof-prints in the area, or other signs of the uni-corn passing through.

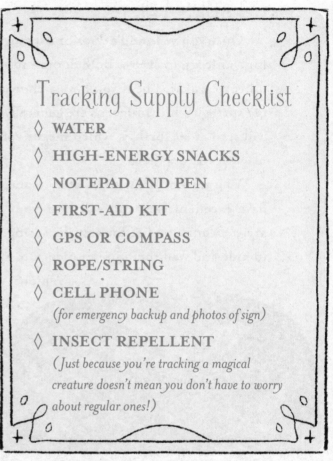

Tracking Supply Checklist

◊ **WATER**

◊ **HIGH-ENERGY SNACKS**

◊ **NOTEPAD AND PEN**

◊ **FIRST-AID KIT**

◊ **GPS OR COMPASS**

◊ **ROPE/STRING**

◊ **CELL PHONE**
  (for emergency backup and photos of sign)

◊ **INSECT REPELLENT**
  (Just because you're tracking a magical creature doesn't mean you don't have to worry about regular ones!)

Is there an established trail nearby? Like most forest animals, a unicorn is likely to follow "goat tracks" or "deer trails"—paths that have been worn down over time and have become commonly used routes for many animals. If not, look for broken twigs or branches, or tufts of white hair* caught on branches nearby. Travel in widen-ing circles around each sign until you find another one. Then start

---

* If you do find a piece of unicorn mane, be sure to hold on to it for making infinite friendship bracelets. See page 142 for instructions.

again. You will eventually establish a trail that will take you back to the unicorn's door or spring.

CREATING A HIDE

Once you've found a door or a spring, you can settle in and wait for a unicorn to arrive. Both doors and springs are likely places for unicorn traffic, but if you have a choice between the two, choose the spring. While unicorns are generally faithful to one door, they will stop at all springs, which means you have a greater chance of magical visitors there.

You are not likely to be able to sneak up on a unicorn. They have excellent ears and will hear your footfalls long before you arrive. Your best bet for actually seeing one is to establish a place to hide and wait there for a unicorn to arrive.

A hide is a structure that is designed to blend in with the forest and provide a place for you to wait without animals seeing you. You can build a hut or lean-to and either paint it forest green (white for snowy locations) or cover it in camouflage fabric. Or you can buy a pop-up tent that is made for that purpose. You can find tutorials and guides on wildlife photography and hunting websites.

Any well-camouflaged hide will work. While unicorns cannot be fooled by magical means, they are often more tuned in to magical deception and can be more easily deceived by human camouflage. But keep in mind while setting up your hideaway that you will be spending a lot of time there. It should be comfortable and have room for you to bring some basic supplies like a comfortable chair, food, water, and a good book.

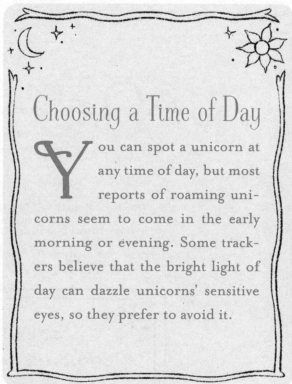

Choosing a Time of Day

You can spot a unicorn at any time of day, but most reports of roaming unicorns seem to come in the early morning or evening. Some trackers believe that the bright light of day can dazzle unicorns' sensitive eyes, so they prefer to avoid it.

This is by far the most difficult part of unicorn tracking, as it requires a lot of patience. You will likely have to spend hours or even days in your hide, keeping silent the entire time so that you won't alert the unicorn to your presence.

If you're quiet and patient enough, however, you may one day be waiting in your hide and hear the snap of a twig as an animal approaches. Moving very slowly and silently, you will set down your book and peek from the window to see a flash of white through the trees. In few more moments, you'll get a clear view—a wild unicorn, pacing majestically toward you. Resist the urge to cry out. Many a unicorn tracker has frightened off the animal by gasping at first sight of it. Maintain your cool, and you'll be one of the very few humans who have been able to observe a unicorn in its habitat!

Camera Traps

Once you've found a good place for observing unicorns, you may be tempted to take the easy way out and set a camera trap. Wildlife cameras—weatherproofed setups that are activated by motion—are a popular way to get photos of shy animals in the wild. Set one up in a remote spot and it will be triggered to snap a picture whenever an animal passes by.

Stakeout Checklist

◊ **BOOKS OR MAGAZINES**

◊ **COMFORTABLE CHAIR**

◊ **NOTEPAD AND PEN**

◊ **CELL PHONE**—*silent mode on—for emergencies (not recommended for listening to music or podcasts, since even the sound of music through headphones might be heard by a cautious unicorn)*

◊ **SNACKS** *(avoid wrappers/bags that might crinkle when you reach into them)*

◊ **WATER**

◊ **WARM CLOTHES/SLEEPING BAG** *as needed (sitting still can get really chilly)*

◊ **FLASHLIGHT**

Of course, you're welcome to try a camera trap, but be warned: No one has ever managed to get a photo of a unicorn, either by camera trap or in person. It is unclear why this is. Photographers report that their cameras mysteriously broke or ran out of charge, or that they managed to take a photo only to find that the unicorn was so blurry in the final image you couldn't tell what it was. It may be that unicorns enjoy magical protection that is similar to fairy glamour. But it's also possible that unicorn photographers have just been extremely unlucky. There's only one way to find out.

CATCHING A UNICORN

It is not a good idea to attempt to capture a unicorn. Despite their gentle appearance, they are still wild animals. Their speed and agility are legend, and their horns can serve as spears if they are cornered. It's fair to say that attempting to capture a massive creature that can outrun you or defend itself with a large, pointy weapon is perilous.

At best, the unicorn will escape. At worst, it will seriously injure you.

IF YOU INSIST

If you are really intent on trying to capture a unicorn, please reread the warning above.

IF YOU REALLY, REALLY INSIST

If you are still determined, despite the obvious pitfalls, there are a few tricks that might (but only *might*) increase your chances of success:

First, you should realize that you will not be able to capture a unicorn by force. In the very unlikely scenario that you are able to catch a creature that can run faster than a Ferrari, or corner it without being gored, you should be aware that a reluctant unicorn is also significantly heavier and harder to move than a horse.

Medieval literature is very clear on the fact that unicorns must be captured willingly. (While it is true that medieval literature is full of a lot of questionable ideas and incredibly bad science, many unicorn trackers believe that there is some truth to this one.)

It is possible to convince a unicorn to come to you. But, of course, there is a catch. Unicorns are attracted to innocence and purity. According to some medieval texts, if a unicorn approached a human and discovered they were not pure, the consequences could be pretty dire. So before you attempt to lure a unicorn, ask yourself this question: Are you pure of heart?

Even if you believe you are, you may want to do some work before you attempt to find a unicorn. Do some soul searching. Meditate. Volunteer work can be good for the soul, too.

The largest horses, Shire Horses, can weigh up to 2,500 pounds. Unicorns, though significantly smaller, can weigh almost twice as much. Since very few unicorns have been captured (and none in modern times), no one has been able to study this phenomenon to understand it. Perhaps if you are successful in catching one, you can run some tests.

Ask yourself *why* you want to capture a unicorn. If your reasons aren't good, you will be doomed from the start.

WHEN YOU'RE READY

If you're feeling confident that you'll pass the unicorn test for good intentions (Are you really sure? It's really important for you to be right on this . . .), you can try to approach a unicorn. Or rather, you can try to convince a unicorn to approach you. If the unicorn sees you coming from a distance, it will bolt long before you get close enough for it to decide whether you are worthy. The trick, then, is to wait for the unicorn in a place that you have already determined it is likely to visit.

Sit quietly and patiently, and for heaven's sake try to look as angelic as you can. If the unicorn sees you and is intrigued enough by you, it will approach. If it feels that you are pure and gentle enough, it will lie down with its head in your lap. (If you don't pass the unicorn test, it will be much less friendly. You may want to have an exit strategy ready, just in case.)

Once it has submitted, the unicorn is yours. It will willingly follow you home.

CATCHING A WINGED UNICORN

Taming a winged unicorn makes a lot more sense than trying to catch an earth-bound one. Along with their wings, flying unicorns inherit many of their personality traits from their mythical ancestor, Pegasus. Most important, they are fairly docile and even enjoy being ridden by the right person. They make much better pets than their wild cousins, and with a little work, you can likely capture one without much danger. But that doesn't mean that catching it will be easy.

Unicorn Hunting Checklist

◊ **COMFORTABLE RUNNING SHOES**

◊ **SUPPLIES FOR WAITING** *in the woods (snacks, water, bug repellent, rain gear, etc.)*

◊ **GOOD INTENTIONS**

While traditional unicorns are wild animals that survive on impulse and instinct, winged unicorns are the thinkers of the unicorn family. You are unlikely to be able to catch one through trickery, as they will quickly think their way through any human deception. They understand human speech and interactions, and make up their own minds about potential human riders.

Like a traditional unicorn, a winged unicorn will only submit to a worthy person. But their idea of what makes a rider acceptable can be far more complicated. Instead of a simple purity test, winged unicorns ask themselves a host of questions about every new human they meet: *Do I like this person? Do they need my help? Do they seem like they would be a good companion on a long flight?*

Taming a winged unicorn is a little like convincing a human to be your friend. You have to put your true self forward and hope for the best.

Try to approach the winged unicorn in an environment where it's likely to be in a good mood—enchanted springs are best for this. Let the winged unicorn take a good, long drink before you approach it.

You should bring an offering. A halter is traditional, but any old halter will not do. Bellerophon wooed Pegasus with an enchanted halter that had been crafted from gold by Athena, the goddess of wisdom, so the bar here is pretty high. Anything with magical properties that might protect or charm the animal wearing it is definitely in the right ballpark.

Obviously, not everyone has access to magical items. If that's just not a realistic possibility in your area, you can try anything fancy—ribbons, jewelry (fake gems are fine, as long as they sparkle!), or intricate needlework. Winged unicorns aren't against a little bling.

Keep in mind that while they are willing to be ridden and even like a little horse tack, a unicorn does not want to wear a bridle and bit. They will take you where you want to go, but *they* decide how to get there. A saddle is not a good way to go, either, since most saddles do not fit well around wings. Stick to a halter, and perhaps a decorative blanket.

Approach the winged unicorn slowly, holding out your offering and talking in low tones. Explain that you would like it to be your steed, but remember that it can understand you. No winged unicorn is going to sign up to be your servant, but it might like the idea of a partnership that features adventures, lots of brushing, hugs, and fresh hay. Keep it simple, along the lines of, "Hi. My name is _____. I hope that you might be interested in being my steed.* Let me tell you a little bit about myself . . ."

If you're not making your case well, you'll know pretty quickly. An unimpressed unicorn will take off and leave you in its dust. But if it is intrigued, it will approach. Take things slowly. Hold the halter up so that the unicorn can investigate. If it makes any moves to put its muzzle in the halter, you're in. Fasten it on and ask permission to ride. At this point, the winged unicorn should bow and allow you to climb on its back.

At no point in the process of meeting the unicorn should you attempt to catch it against its will. Although a winged unicorn is far less dangerous than a regular unicorn, it is still a magical, armed creature that will easily overpower you if angered. If it seems reluctant or begins to back away, let it go. You can always try again with another winged unicorn.

CARE AND FEEDING

Before you bring home a unicorn, you should be prepared to care for it. Like any other pet, they need a safe place to sleep and play, fresh water and treats, and proper grooming and affection. But don't make the mistake of assuming that your unicorn is just a horse in disguise. Like all animals, they have very specific needs. You'll have to set up an environment that is specially tailored for your new pet. Here are a few tips to help you prepare.

SHELTER

Both unicorns and their winged cousins will remain with you

---

* Please take care to avoid calling the unicorn a horse. If you had a horn and wings, how would you feel about being called a horse? It's kind of like calling a full-grown lion a kitty cat. It can be kind of cute, I guess, but it's more likely to be taken as an insult.

as long as you continue to hold up your half of the partnership. Finding a place to keep them, then, is less about keeping them contained than it is about making them happy.

Neither unicorns nor winged unicorns like being kept indoors. They can appreciate a warm, dry area, and even enjoy chomping on fresh hay now and again, but as wild animals, they do not do well with a roof and concrete or wooden floors, so stables and barns are out. Whenever possible, keep them in an open meadow. A paddock or outdoor ring is the next best thing. If neither is possible, follow these guidelines to establish a good home:

UNICORNS

Your challenge is to create an environment that will please the unicorn and encourage it to stay with you. Unicorns are used to having free range and will be uneasy in an enclosed space. A typical horse fence is fine, but keep in mind that it is just for show. Any unicorn can jump over a standard horse fence. Full walls are not recommended. A unicorn will, however, make use of an open-sided shelter if it is free to come and go as it pleases.

WINGED UNICORNS

Since their first response to any danger is to take to the air, a winged unicorn will not enter any space that has a roof. Their thick coat is extremely warm and waterproof, capable of weathering the extremes of high altitudes, so they do not require shelter, although they will appreciate the shade of trees during the summer months.

A winged unicorn will weather a typical thunder or snowstorm by waiting it out with its head under a wing. In the event of hurricanes or tornadoes, the unicorn will likely take off for someplace where the weather is less dangerous. (You may want to consider going with it.) Don't worry, it will return when it is safe.

A winged unicorn will appreciate an area where the ground is dry, preferably with a thick layer of hay to bed down in. In urban environments, a rooftop garden may be passable. Create an outdoor space that focuses on natural beauty: healthy grass and flowers, fountains and waterfalls, and tasteful sculpture can all go a long way to making a winged unicorn feel at home.

FOOD AND WATER

Your primary job as a unicorn keeper is to act like a generous host. Shower your unicorn with care and you'll both be much happier in the long run.

Unicorns love to drink water, and lots of it. While it isn't technically necessary to provide them with clean water, since they can instantly purify it with their horns, leaving your unicorn with a

mucky puddle isn't going to make it feel welcomed. Ideally, you'll want to give them water in a form that mimics the natural springs they prefer. If there happens to be a spring or brook nearby, build your unicorn habitat around it. A circulating pond or fountain would be the next best thing. If you must resort to using a trough or bucket for water, dig a hole and set it into the ground. Disguise the edges with rocks and plants, and refill it with fresh water at least twice a day.

It may surprise you to learn that your unicorn will not need food to survive. It is assumed that they eat when in the magical realm, but they are not known to need food when they are in ours. While this phenomenon is poorly understood, most unicorn trackers agree that it has something to do with differences in the passage of time between the two worlds. Days, and even weeks, in this world translate to minutes in their own. It's assumed, then, that their bodies are set to a different clock.

But just because a unicorn doesn't need food doesn't mean it won't appreciate a snack. Like horses, unicorns are partial to sweet, crunchy snacks, and you should provide them with a steady supply of tasty treats to keep them happy.

Fresh hay and oats are nice for absentminded munching. A meadow full of spring grass and clover takes things to the next level. But if you want to make sure your magical friend sticks around, you'll need to lay on the treats. Homemade horse cookies are a good way to go, but bear in mind that unicorns have an unusually sweet tooth. If the recipe calls for molasses or honey, double it. Feed treats like sugar cubes and mints freely. Sprinkle brown sugar and maple syrup into oats.

You can pretty much feel free to feed your unicorn any sweet treat that it desires, since their magical systems do not seem to be affected by the kinds of foods that might harm horses. But stick to vegan items. Hard candies and chocolates are a definite yes, but marshmallows or other gelatin-based candy might send the wrong message.

POOP

If you've ever cared for a horse, you know that maintaining a stable involves shoveling *a lot* of poop. You may be getting out your wellies and preparing to do the same for your unicorn. It seems indelicate to mention it in reference to such a noble, magical beast, but since the question is bound to arise: You can put away your wellies, but keep your shovel handy.

A creature that doesn't need to eat has little need for other bodily functions. (At least when they're in our world. There is no definitive word on what they do in theirs.) In extremely rare cases, you may find some magic meadow muffins in your unicorn enclosure. Treat them with respect. Unicorn poop is the finest known fertilizer in the world. A shovelful of the stuff will boost a field as big as a city block. And when I say boost, I mean *turbo* boost. Spread thinly in a garden, it will accelerate plant growth at a rate that outpaces Jack's magic beanstalk.

GROOMING

If you haven't figured it out yet, caring for a unicorn is all about pampering. And nothing pampers an equine more than a good grooming session.

You'll want to have a good grooming kit ready and be prepared to use it every day. Grooming is a great way to bond with your unicorn. It is also essential to help manage a unicorn's thick coat.

Unicorns shed. A lot. Their coat is much thicker than regular horses' and does not shed in cycles. It continuously renews itself, growing new hair and dropping old on a daily basis. Unicorns who are passing continuously in and out of Faerie seem to maintain a naturally groomed coat. It's possible that living in their preferred time cycle slows the rate of hair growth, or it may be that they are groomed by other means—perhaps by other unicorns—when they are with the herd in the magical realm.

A unicorn that is kept in the non-magical world, however,

can quickly develop mats as shed hair tangles with the new coat, and they're also known to pick up burrs and seeds as they run through the woods. Winged unicorns have their own hazards—it's not uncommon for them to pick up feathers and bird mites from communing with airborne flocks. The cold, damp weather at altitude can also coat the hair, mane, and tale with clumps of ice and packed snow.

After a long ride in the clouds or on the snowy ground, your unicorn will appreciate a warm soapy bath. Rub it down using a sponge and a bucket of warm water mixed with an unscented horse shampoo. Rinse using warm water, too. Your unicorn will not appreciate being hosed down. Towel the unicorn dry—not because they need it, but because it feels good!

On a daily basis, you'll need to groom the unicorn much like you would a horse. Make sure you have a good, soft currycomb and a stiff brush. Work the currycomb in a circular motion to loosen dirt, burrs, and loose hair from the coat. Take your time doing this, and use the opportunity to bond with your unicorn. You'll probably notice its unusual smell—many people who have been close to them insist that unicorns smell like angel food cake or cotton candy. This may be the result of their sugar-heavy diets. But others think that unicorn smell is closer to wild mint and thyme, so it may also be dependent on where your unicorn prefers to roll.

While you're brushing, talk soothingly to the unicorn. Always remember that it can understand you—baby talk and gibberish won't be appreciated. But compliments are always well received, as are news and gossip. Also, while unicorns are tough animals, they are also exceedingly ticklish. Be extremely cautious around the traditional tickle spots: under the legs and on the belly.

Once you've curried the unicorn, brush it with a good stiff brush to remove the loose hair and dirt. You can then work on its mane and tail.

Due to unicorns' magical properties, you will not be able to trim knots out of a unicorn's mane and tail, but combing and braiding them will be appreciated. Use a wide-toothed comb to carefully remove burrs, knots, or ice from the mane, tail, and forelock.

It is a good idea to braid the unicorn's mane and tail. It helps prevent them from picking up brambles, but unicorns are also a bit vain and will really appreciate looking fancy. Consider weaving in flowers or ribbons to win extra points with your friend.

NEVER TOUCH THE UNICORN'S HORN!
THE HORN IS THE SOURCE OF THE UNICORN'S
POWER, AND IT IS A SERIOUS BREACH OF
UNICORN ETIQUETTE TO TOUCH IT.

You do not need to worry about the unicorn's hooves, since their magical properties keep them pristine. Nor is it recommended that you attempt to groom the wings of a winged unicorn. You *can* gently run your fingers through the 'corn's feathers, and pick out any loose feathers or obvious twigs. But the unicorn will mostly maintain its own wings. Be on the lookout, though, for signs of bird mites. If your unicorn seems to be biting at its wings or rubbing them up against trees more often than usual, contact a veterinarian.

How to Create a Running Braid

A running braid is a great way to keep a unicorn's mane out of trouble. (It's also excellent for humans! See page 136 for instructions.)

1. Start at the top of the mane as though you will be starting a regular braid: Grab a section of hair and divide it into three pieces.
2. Make one plait, beginning with the right strand and taking each of the three outside pieces to the center of the braid.
3. Before beginning the second plait, take another section of hair from the mane on the left and add it to the left side of the braid. Take it to the middle as you would with a normal braid.

4. When it's time to bring the right strand to the middle, do not pick up any more hair. Just bring it to the center as it is.
5. Continue down the mane, angling the braid slowly away from the top of the neck.
6. When you run out of mane to add to the braid, continue with a standard braid until all the hair is bound.
7. Use a ponytail holder to hold the braid together.

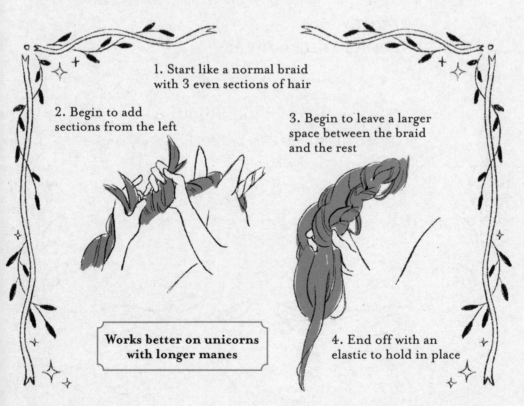

1. Start like a normal braid with 3 even sections of hair

2. Begin to add sections from the left

3. Begin to leave a larger space between the braid and the rest

Works better on unicorns with longer manes

4. End off with an elastic to hold in place

Grooming Supply Checklist

◊ **CURRY COMB** *(soft rubber)*

◊ **STIFF BRUSH** *(use sparingly to avoid arguments)*

◊ **SOFT BRUSH**

◊ **GROOMING TOWEL**

◊ **WIDE-TOOTHED COMB**

◊ **NATURAL, UNSCENTED HORSE SHAMPOO**
(You may add natural oils for perfume, but unicorns detest chemical perfumes.)

◊ **RIBBONS AND FLOWERS** *for braiding*

Not recommended:

◊ **SHEDDING BLADE** *(its hard metal teeth are often taken the wrong way by the unicorn)*

◊ **TRIMMING SCISSORS** *(ineffective on magical hair)*

◊ **HOOF PICK** *(unnecessary on magical hooves)*

UNICORN GAMES

You didn't go to the trouble to track and capture a unicorn just so you could carry water and change bedding for it. When most people imagine life with a unicorn, their fantasy includes riding through sun-kissed meadows or flying through the clouds. Unicorns are the fastest of land animals, and winged unicorns add the possibility of flight. It's only natural to want to spend time running and playing with your new companion.

Unicorns can make excellent playmates and there are a lot of great activities you can share with them. Be creative—unicorns' intelligence and curiosity make them suitable for a wide range of games. But, just like everything else, play is a bit different with these magical creatures than it is with a horse. You'll need to keep the rules and restrictions of unicorns in mind when you play.

RIDING

Of course you want to ride your unicorn! Their incredible speed and unusually smooth gait are perfect for it. But is it a good idea? Bear in mind that unicorns are essentially wild animals. The fact that you have captured one does not mean that you have completely tamed it. You have only managed to hold its ferocity in check for a while. Let it run and you may get more than you bargained for.

Since unicorns are so high-spirited, it is not a good idea to make one your first riding experience. You'll need years of practice on horses before you can begin to ride a unicorn safely. If you are an experienced rider and want to go for it, make sure that you wear proper safety gear. You'll definitely need a helmet, and you might want to consider some kind of padding or body armor, too. Remember that your unicorn can travel at speeds that are far, far faster than the average horse. You'll need to be prepared to take the kind of fall that you might experience from a racing motorcycle. A very tall racing motorcycle.

You should also have plenty of practice in riding bareback. Unicorns will not tolerate a saddle or bit, although depending on yours, you may be able to tie a strap around the base of its neck to help with stability.

Also keep in mind that you will not be in control of your direction or speed. Riding a unicorn is an exercise in learning to let go. If you succeed in getting onto your unicorn's back, it will not take directions. It will go where it pleases and for as long as it pleases. Your job is simply to stay on and try to enjoy the ride.

Bareback Basics

Riding bareback requires excellent balance. You will not have a saddle or stirrups to help you stay on the unicorn's back. Here are a few tips from the pros that might help keep you seated:

◊ SIT UP STRAIGHT. Many people tend to slouch without a saddle, which can make it harder to maintain balance. Keep your body straight through your core.

◊ KEEP YOUR LEGS below your body, where they would sit if you were riding properly in a saddle.

◊ YOU WILL NEED strong legs. Make sure that you have spent sufficient time riding to build up muscle memory and strength.

◊ **KEEP A LOOSE** hip. Although your legs should be engaged, your torso needs to be able to stay balanced and straight despite the movement of the unicorn's back. Let your hips swivel while the rest of your body stays strong.

◊ **DON'T BE AFRAID** to take hold of the unicorn's mane for help with balance. Or, if your unicorn's willing, you can try attaching a strap around the base of its neck to provide a handhold.

◊ **JUST BECAUSE YOU'RE** riding without a saddle, that doesn't mean you should skip the safety equipment. Always wear a helmet, even if you're giving up the stirrups.

Grip mane gently for balance

Sit farther forward, between shoulder and barrel

Allow your weight to shift from side to side with each step

Sit upright

MOUNTING A UNICORN

It can be difficult to climb onto a barebacked animal, and a unicorn will not stand placidly by a fence or mounting block while you clamber onto it. Your best bet is to get the unicorn to lie on the ground.

Remember back when you originally met? Your unicorn lay down and put its head in your lap. In order to ride it, you'll need to get it to do so again. If you've been taking proper care of it, providing it with treats, fresh water, and lots and lots of rubdowns, this should be relatively easy. Sit quietly on the ground and wait for your unicorn to approach. Talk softly or sing, and stroke its muzzle gently. It should lie down and place its head in your lap. Once it has done so, you may climb onto its back. Keep your movements slow and your voice gentle.

If you have not been taking proper care of your unicorn, do not attempt this! Unicorns are not above trickery. It may allow you onto its back just so it can have the opportunity to throw you off.

MAKE SURE THAT YOU ARE WEARING PROPER SAFETY EQUIPMENT. A HELMET IS A MUST!

MOUNTING A WINGED UNICORN

Mounting and riding a winged unicorn is much easier. You can start by putting on a halter, but ask permission first. Explain that you would like to ride it and that the halter might be helpful. If you've developed a good rapport with the unicorn, it might even nod to give permission. If it hasn't yet learned human communication, hold the halter up and wait for the unicorn to put its nose in. At that point, you can feel free to buckle it on. If you have a really tolerant unicorn, you might even want to try attaching a lead rope to the halter and looping it around the unicorn's neck to form reins.

You can likely get the unicorn to stand next to a mounting block or stepladder and let you climb onto its back. You can also try asking it to bow or lie down. Just make sure that you communicate what you want clearly, and that you remember to thank the unicorn at every step. Manners matter.

Deciding where to sit on a winged unicorn can be especially tricky. Most people choose to sit behind the wings. Look for the joint where the wing attaches to the body. There should be a few inches of short feathers there, before they begin to spread and fill out the rest of the wing. Move forward until your thighs fit snugly into this gap.

But there are some disadvantages to sitting behind the wings, most of which won't be obvious until you're underway. You will find that they rub your legs as they move up and down, which, over time, can cause chafing. Sitting behind the wings also means that you are in their air wash. Along with the wind created by flying at high speeds, you will also feel the wind created by the fanning action of two enormous wings. And this position places you farther from the unicorn's neck, making it harder to hold its mane or use reins.

For this reason, many riders prefer to sit in front of the wings, although this creates its own problems. While there is a relatively safe and even place for riding directly between the wings, sitting there requires that you keep your legs forward, making it difficult to maintain balance. DO NOT ATTEMPT THIS POSITION. If you want to try riding in front of the wings, you will need to ride far forward, almost over the shoulders. This is not a natural seat for an experienced rider, but some prefer it.

Once you've found your seat, you can certainly ask your steed to take you where you want to go, or try using reins to turn its head. But keep in mind that these are only suggestions. Your unicorn will ultimately decide where to take you. Try to relax and enjoy the ride.

MAKE SURE THAT YOU ARE WEARING PROPER SAFETY EQUIPMENT. YOU WILL NEED COLD-WEATHER GEAR, EVEN IF IT IS WARM AT GROUND LEVEL. YOU WON'T BE ABLE TO PUT THEM ON WHILE YOU'RE FLYING, SO START OUT WITH A COAT, GLOVES, AND THERMAL LAYERS ALREADY ON. A HELMET IS A MUST. A PARACHUTE IS ALSO A GOOD IDEA.

SPORTS

Once you have learned to ride your unicorn, it can be tempting to join in competitions. This is not recommended. While unicorns are competitive and enjoy playing games, they are still wild animals with horns and could accidentally inflict harm on their competition. That being said, they will enjoy practicing these sports alone with you. You may want to try one of the following:

STEEPLECHASE/
CROSS-COUNTRY EQUESTRIAN COURSES Their skill and speed while navigating in the woods make unicorns natural steeplechasers. Winged unicorns, however, may take to the air when they encounter the first jump.

SOCCER Both winged and land-bound unicorns will appreciate kicking around a large beach or Pilates ball. Make sure that you have extra balls handy, since inflated balls and sharp horns don't mix well, and a disappointed unicorn is no joke.

VAULTING A unicorn's incredibly smooth stride and wry sense of humor make it an ideal partner for practicing vaulting routines. If you are into gymnastics, this could be a great activity for you. The horn does pose an added hazard in case of tumbles. If your unicorn is winged, make sure that it is willing to stay on the ground, since performing handstands above the treetops is perilous.

SWIMMING/DIVING Unicorns are excellent natural swimmers. While they love the water, they are not particularly *fast* swimmers, which makes swimming and diving rare opportunities for you to actually beat them in competition. But they can be sore losers and they are armed, so resist the urge to gloat.

HIDE-AND-SEEK Unicorns are naturals when it comes to hiding. It's possible that magic plays a role in their ability to camouflage themselves in the woods. You will never be able to find them, and they will always find you. But games of hide-and-seek can be a great way to bolster your relationship—and your unicorn's ego.

MAGICAL PURSUITS

The magical world is always present. Magical creatures lurk in ancient forests. Some may even make their way into cities and suburbs, hiding in plain sight. It's likely that you'll never see them—their doorways and homes are shielded from humans by magical glamours and mists.

But your unicorn is always tuned in to the magical realm. As creatures of that world, they can identify every fairy and sprite—every magical doorway and cursed object. When you brought home your unicorn, you gained a partner in magical adventure. You can tap into your unicorn's magical abilities for everything from jewel hunting and unicorn tracking to humanitarian work. Your imagination is the only limit to what you can do, but keep in mind one rule. Your unicorn made a decision about your character when it agreed to become your pet. It will trust you and share its magical skills. But don't get greedy—use them for the wrong reasons and your unicorn may stop helping you, or even decide that it's time to move on.

TRACKING

Remember those long weeks, months, and years you put into tracking your new friend? The days you spent trekking through the woods looking for a unicorn door? The long hours you spent following a hint of a trail only to find that it was just a deer track?

Now that you actually have a unicorn, you can find another without any of that fuss. Your unicorn will gladly lead you to any nearby unicorn door, and to the local enchanted spring, too! And the fact that your unicorn is with you will go a long way to convincing another unicorn that you're okay.

You are now tapped into the unicorn world and can easily find more and more. But before you get any ideas about building a herd, you should know that not all unicorns appreciate competition. They'll help you track other unicorns, but they may react badly to bringing new ones home. Winged unicorns, who are known to flock, may be more happy to have new friends, but proceed with caution.

Your buddy can lead you to a Faerie door and that means you will be able to track magical creatures of all kinds. Unicorns and fairies are only a few of the creatures that pass through the average portal. This is your golden opportunity to meet a leprechaun, spot a phoenix, or glimpse a dragon (hopefully from a distance).

Ask your unicorn to lead you to a doorway and wait to see who comes through. Even on a slow day, one or two magical creatures are likely to come along. Be patient. And whatever you do, do not attempt to pass through a unicorn door to Faerie. This has never ended well for a human.

TREASURE HUNTING

Unicorns love bling, and they have an excellent nose for it. Think of them a bit like bloodhounds. (But never, never call your unicorn a dog to its face.)

When you were tracking your unicorn, you may have found fields of magical crystals that it dug up. Unicorns have an affinity for magical stones, but they can also sniff out gold, silver, semiprecious stones, and gems. Let your unicorn roam without instructions, and it will soon turn up any precious metals or jewels that can be found in the area. Buried treasure, undiscovered silver and gold deposits, lost jewelry—you name it, and your unicorn will find it. You can even sit by while it digs the treasure up. But be aware that your unicorn won't take kindly to your swooping in at the last minute and trying to pocket all of its findings. It's a good idea to let your unicorn keep most of what it finds, especially if it's something the unicorn can wear, such as a necklace or bracelet. But ask politely (and throw in some flattery) and your unicorn may let you take some of its treasure home.

WATER CONNING Your new friend isn't just useful to you—it's a potential boon to humanity, too. There's enough magic in its horn to clean up all the water on earth.

Consider, then, sharing its powers with others. Polluted water is a real problem for people and wildlife alike. Your unicorn only needs to dip its horn into any stream, lake, or ocean to rid it of poisonous chemicals. Unicorns have been known to purify watering holes for other animals for centuries, and there's no reason they should stop now.

No one is sure exactly how far an alicorn's magic will go with one dip. It can purify a well, a river, a lake. But if you dip into an ocean, could it purify the entire thing at once? All the earth's oceans are really one giant connected system—would it purify all of them?

Don't you want to find out?

Unicorn Your Life

There's more than one way to indulge your inner unicorn. Write your own legends. Share the joy with rainbows and sparkles. Wear your unicornimania on your sleeve. There are a million and one ways for a crafty, resourceful unicorn lover to share the joy. You may not have one in your backyard, but you can still keep unicorns in your everyday life.

BRAIDS GALORE

Want to show a little unicorn solidarity? Braid that mane! Throw in a rainbow of ribbons to kick things up to unicorn level. You can create any of these styles with or without the extra color. If you don't have ribbon handy, just skip the steps that mention them and you'll still wind up with a fantastic braid.

KEEP IT SIMPLE, SISTER

You can unicorn the most basic braid simply by adding colored ribbon. Cloth ribbon works best, but in a pinch you can use curling ribbon (the kind you'd use with wrapping paper). It's a little harder to work with, but still looks great! Try wide ribbons for a funky look, or narrow ones if you just want to add some color. You can also add more ribbons by tying one to each piece of hair.

YOU'LL NEED:
◊ A brush or comb
◊ A ribbon about twice as long as your hair
◊ A ponytail holder

STEP 1: Divide the hair you want to braid into three pieces.

STEP 2: Take a ribbon about twice the length of the hair and loop it around to the top of the middle piece. Make sure the ends of the ribbon are about the same length.

STEP 3: Take the right-hand piece of hair along with one end of the ribbon in your right hand, and the left-hand piece of hair along with the other end of the ribbon in your left.

STEP 4: Cross the right-hand piece of hair and ribbon over the middle piece of hair to the middle of the braid.

STEP 5: Do the same with the left-hand piece of hair and ribbon.

STEP 6: Continue to the end of the hair, moving pieces from the right-hand position to the middle and then from the left-hand position to the middle. Move the ribbons along with the pieces of hair they started with.

STEP 7: Fasten the hair and ribbons together with a ponytail holder at the end of the braid. If needed, use scissors to trim any overly long pieces of ribbon. (Be careful not to cut the hair!)

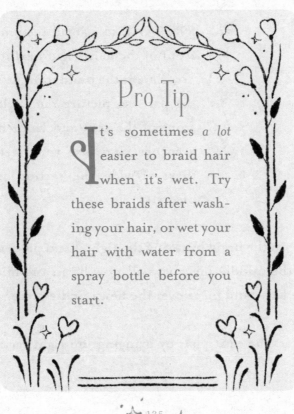

Pro Tip

It's sometimes *a lot* easier to braid hair when it's wet. Try these braids after washing your hair, or wet your hair with water from a spray bottle before you start.

RUNNING BRAID

Nothing says "I'm with you" like matching hairstyles. You can use the human version of the running braid to tame your own locks. This style works a little better with a side part, which gives you a longer run of braid, but if a middle part is your thing, that's fine, too. Also, these instructions are for a braid on the right side of the part. To create one on the left, you'll need to reverse the rights and lefts below!

How does this work on a mane? See page 119 for the equine version.

YOU'LL NEED:
◊ A brush or comb
◊ A ponytail holder

STEP 1: Take a small section from the front of the hair, right next to the part. You'll want the braid to angle away from the part, so picture the angle between front of the part and front hairline as a corner, and take your section from there. Divide the section into three pieces.

STEP 2: Begin the braid by taking the right-hand piece and crossing it over the middle piece (it will now be in the middle) and crossing the left-hand piece over the new middle piece.

STEP 3: Start the next plait by bringing the right section to the middle.

STEP 4: Pick up a new piece of hair, about the same size as the pieces of the braid, from along the part, right behind the beginning section, and combine it with the left piece of the braid. Move the new hair, along with the left-hand piece, to the center of the braid.

STEP 5: Continue in the same manner, moving diagonally from the part. You should continue to cross the right-hand side of the braid to the middle without adding to it, but pick up new pieces of hair from the left, until you reach the end of the part.

STEP 6: Continue with a basic braid to the end of the hair and secure with a ponytail holder.

A ROMANTIC TWIST

Unicorn maidens should have the most romantic tresses. If you want to release your inner medieval princess, try this regal style.

YOU'LL NEED:
◊ A brush or comb
◊ Colorful ribbons—one big enough to tie around your head, and several more that are about the same length as your hair
◊ Ponytail holder

STEP 1: Create a crown—run one ribbon around your head so that it forms a loop. It should sit a couple of inches from the front of the hair and an inch or two above the ears. Tie the ends together in the back and trim any excess.

STEP 2: Tie the ends of several ribbons to the crown, beginning about even with the ears and spacing them evenly around the back. (This is going to look really goofy. Don't worry, it looks better later.)

STEP 3: With the crown in place, begin the twist. Pick up a section of hair from the front, loop it through the top of the crown, and pull it completely through. Pull tight.

STEP 4: Work your way from front to back on one side, looping sections of hair from the front up and over the crown and pulling it through. When you loop over one of the dangling ribbons, incorporate them into the hair on the next loop.

STEP 5: Stop when you reach the middle of the crown in the back. Check that the crown and ribbons are all neatly covered.

STEP 6: Repeat steps 3–5 on the other side.

STEP 7: When both twists have reached the back of the crown (they should meet in the middle), divide the hair and ribbons at the back into three pieces and braid.

STEP 8: Fasten the braid and ribbon ends with a ponytail holder. You can trim any loose ribbon ends with scissors, but be careful not to cut the hair.

BOX IT UP!

What's better than a braid? A whole lot of braids! This great style takes some time, but in the end you'll wind up with ten times the unicorn power. Get creative with your braid hair to weave in a rainbow of colors.

YOU'LL NEED:
◊ A brush and comb
◊ Styling clips
◊ Braiding hair (You can choose one that matches your hair color or try rainbow colors for the full unicorn look.)
◊ Long lengths of paracord or thick, colored string
◊ Ponytail holders

STEP 1: Create the box pattern—clip most of the hair up onto the top of the head, leaving the back loose. Use the comb to form a horizontal part across the bottom of the hair. (Where you put this part will determine how big the boxes are. The larger the boxes, the fewer braids you will have in the end. As a general rule, an inch is probably a good amount to start with.) Clip all of the hair above the part up and out of the way, and then make a series of vertical parts across the bottom section to create squares.

STEP 2: Prepare the braid hair—lay the braiding hair on the table and gently tug to get rid of the blunt ends. Or hold one end of the braiding hair with one hand while gently tugging the ends with the other.

STEP 3: Add braid hair to your first braid—separate a section of the braid hair and measure it. It's up to you how thick you want your braids to be—the more braid hair you use, the thicker the braids—but you should use something to measure against so the braids will be a consistent size. Hold the section of braid hair up against one of your fingers or another object to judge its thickness and use the same object to measure for each braid. To add the hair to your braid, first fold it in half to find the middle. Then thread the natural hair down through the fold. (Do this right up near the scalp.) Cross the front of the folded braiding hair over and behind the back fold.

STEP 4: Braid—you should have three strands now, the two ends of the braiding hair and the original section of natural hair. These will form the three strands of the braid. When you crossed the first piece of braiding hair behind the other, you began the plait. Put that first piece into the middle of the three strands, then take the section of the natural hair and cross it behind the middle strand to put it in the middle position. Make sure the braiding hair is snug and tight, then continue to braid, crossing the outside pieces behind the middle piece to take the middle position, alternating left and right. As you continue to braid, slowly lengthen the natural hair section by picking up strands of the braiding hair and adding it to the natural hair section every time you move it to the middle. Fasten the end with a ponytail holder.

STEP 5: Braid some more! When you have finished the first braid, follow the same steps to braid all of the sections you created across the bottom of the scalp. Then, start another row by creating another horizontal part to form a section the same width as the one below and dividing it into squares. Continue around the head, keeping the hair that you are not working with pinned back with the styling clips.

STEP 6: Add some color—when you have finished all the braids (Whew! That was a lot of braiding!), you can add a pop of color by crisscrossing the paracord or colored string around some of the braids. Tie the middle of the string around the top of the braid so that lengths of the two ends are roughly even and the knot is hidden underneath. Bring the two ends to the front of the braid, then cross them in the front before moving them to the back. Cross them in the back, then bring the ends to the front. Keep moving down the braid until you reach the bottom, then tuck the ends of the string under the ponytail holder.

INFINITE FRIENDSHIP

What do you do with that piece of unicorn tail you found on your tracking expedition? Make it into a magical bracelet to cement a friendship or love!

Crafting with unicorn hair can be a real challenge since it can't be trimmed to length, but this fisherman's braid loops back on itself to create an infinite circle. You can braid it right onto your friend's wrist to create an unbreakable bond. Or loop it over a broom handle while you're working—just make sure that you make it big enough to pass over your buddy's hand.

YOU'LL NEED:

◊ One piece of unicorn hair (or paracord), about 5 feet long.

STEP 1: Fold the cord in half, making sure that the two halves are even.

STEP 2: Hold the folded end in one hand about an inch from the fold, creating a loop.

STEP 3: Keeping the loop side up, run the loose ends underneath and around the wrist or broomstick, coming back up behind it.

STEP 4: Thread the loose ends through the front of the loop. Pull the right-hand end outward underneath the right side of the bracelet and the left-hand end outward underneath the left side of the bracelet. You should now have four parallel cords to begin your weave: the two fixed cords of the bracelet and the two loose ends of the cord.

STEP 5: Adjust the bracelet to the tightness you would like, but not too tight! You will need room to pass the cords underneath the bracelet as you braid, and to tie a simple knot on the underside of the bracelet when you are done.

STEP 6: Take the loose cord from the right. Pass it over the right cord of the bracelet and behind the left cord of the bracelet and pull it all the way through.

STEP 7: Take the loose cord from the left. Pass it over the left cord of the bracelet and the loose right cord that you just wove through, and underneath the right cord of the bracelet. Pull it through. The two loose cords should now have switched sides.

STEP 8: Take the loose cord that is now on the right and begin again: Pass it over the right cord of the bracelet, behind the left cord of the bracelet, and pull it all the way through. Then take the loose cord from the left and pass it over the left cord of the bracelet *and* the loose cord you just wove through, then under the right cord of the bracelet. After each weave, push the plait up toward the loop at the top of the bracelet to form a tight fisherman's braid.

STEP 9: Continue around the wrist until you run out of room for weaving. You should have an unbroken braid that goes all the way around the bracelet. Thread the loose ends at the end of the last plait through the outer curves of the first plait. Tie a knot on the underside of the bracelet. If you are using paracord, trim any extra cord. (If you are using unicorn hair, you will not be able to trim it—here's hoping it's not too long.)

WEAR A 'CORN

Part of the fun of spending time with unicorns is imagining yourself as part of the magical world. Who wouldn't want to spend some time in Equestria with Twilight Sparkle, Princess Celestia, and Rarity, or to leap through a unicorn door to Faerie? If only you had a horn . . .

Why not make yourself one? Try these two crafts to turn yourself into a unicorn.

CARTOON HORN

This softer, friendlier horn is perfect for goofing around or for sharing with little kids.

YOU'LL NEED:
◊ Ruler
◊ Marker

◊ Felt or fabric

◊ Fabric scissors

◊ Hot glue gun or a needle and thread in a color to match the felt

◊ Cotton batting or cotton balls

◊ Thin ribbon or embroidery floss for creating a spiral, about 10 inches long

◊ Ribbon, string, or elastic for headband

◊ An adult to help

STEP 1: Create your template

Using a ruler and marker, draw a template on a piece of paper. Begin by drawing a straight line that is 7 inches long. Measure in 2½ inches from on end, and make a mark. Then measure 6½ inches out from your mark, perpendicular from your line, and make another mark. Do the same starting at the other end of your original line. Using the ruler as a straight edge, connect the dots of your quadrilateral. Cut out your template.

STEP 2: Cut the fabric

Place the template on the felt or fabric and draw around it. Cut out the shape.

Cut out a circle that is about 3 inches in diameter.

STEP 3: Form the horn

If you are using a hot glue gun, ask an adult to help you (they're called HOT glue guns for a reason!). Have them run a line of glue along one of the diagonal edges of the felt or fabric. Curl the felt or fabric into a cone shape, overlapping the edges by ½ inch. (Make sure the point is closed.) Allow to dry for five minutes.

If you are sewing your horn, fold the felt shape in half. Sandwich the spiral ribbon inside the halves, so that about a quarter of it is coming out of the top of the horn and the rest is coming out of the bottom. Sew up the open side, angling toward the folded side of the top, so that it comes to a point (you might also need an adult's help). Trim the flat top at an angle so that it will form a point. Turn inside out.

STEP 4: Stuff the horn and close

Fill with cotton balls or batting. If you're using cotton balls, pull them into wispy bits first to avoid lumpy stuffing.

Have an adult run a ring of hot glue around the edge of the felt or fabric circle, and place the open end of the horn on top of it. Pinch to seal the bottom edge of the horn to the outer edge of the circle. Allow glue to dry for five minutes.

Sew around the edge of the circle to seal it to the bottom of the horn. Trim off any excess.

STEP 5: Form the spiral

Using glue, tack the end of the spiral ribbon to the tip of the horn. Allow the glue to dry for a few minutes, then spiral the ribbon around the horn, pulling tightly so that it creates grooves. Glue the end down, trim extra, and adjust to even out the spirals.

If you are sewing, the top end of your ribbon should already be attached to the top of the horn. Follow the spiraling instructions above, tacking the end of the ribbon to the lip around the bottom of the horn.

STEP 6: Attach horn to headband

Center horn on the headband and glue or sew.

FANCY HORN

You can turn modeling clay into an elegant horn, perfect for impressing just about anyone.

YOU'LL NEED:

◊ Polymer clay or air-drying clay

◊ Butter knife or clay knife

◊ Poster board or other lightweight, flexible cardboard

◊ Gems, jewels, or glitter for decorating

◊ Ribbon or headband for attaching the horn to your head

◊ Hot glue gun (plus an adult to help!)

STEP 1: Make the horn

Take two equal-sized pieces of clay, and roll them between your palm and the surface of a table to form two matching long, thin cones. Twist the cones together to form one spiraling horn. Gently roll the horn on the tabletop to smooth out the spiral, and pinch the point so that it is sharp.

Clean up the wide end by cutting off any bits that stick out and pressing the end against a tabletop to even it out.

Bake following manufacturer's instructions (for polymer clay) or air-dry (for air-drying clay).

STEP 2: Make the base

Cut a shape out of poster board to form the base of the horn. You can use any shape (may I suggest a star?), but it should be larger than the bottom of the horn. Decorate with jewels or glitter and attach ribbon to form a headband. You can also attach your horn directly to a premade headband.

STEP 3: Combine

Once your horn has been baked and cooled, have an adult apply a large dollop of hot glue to the bottom and attach it to the base. Hold in place for a few minutes, then allow to cool for several minutes more before wearing.

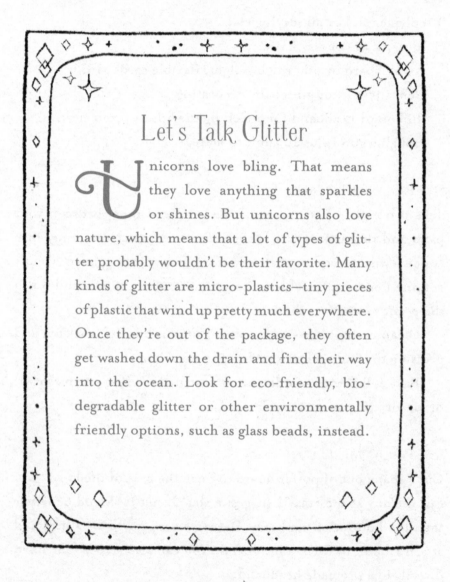

Let's Talk Glitter

Unicorns love bling. That means they love anything that sparkles or shines. But unicorns also love nature, which means that a lot of types of glitter probably wouldn't be their favorite. Many kinds of glitter are micro-plastics—tiny pieces of plastic that wind up pretty much everywhere. Once they're out of the package, they often get washed down the drain and find their way into the ocean. Look for eco-friendly, biodegradable glitter or other environmentally friendly options, such as glass beads, instead.

RAINBOW EVERYTHING

Sometime in the 1980s, unicorns and rainbows became a pair. If you came across a unicorn, you could be pretty sure there was a rainbow nearby. Before long, rainbows started to be almost as much a symbol of unicorns as their horns. Swirl some color into your daily life to pay tribute to all those unicorns who dance somewhere over the rainbow.

MARBLE IT

Marbling is the art of swirling ink or paint on the surface of water, then transferring the design onto paper. The technique has been around since at least the twelfth century, and has been used to make some incredibly beautiful art.

Today, you can still follow the old techniques to create beautiful artwork. But you can also use this modern shortcut to make colorful paper to hang on your wall, trim into invitations and thank-you cards, or use as wrapping paper and book covers. Heavy, absorbent stock such as watercolor paper tends to work best for this craft, but you can use pretty much any paper as long as it isn't glossy.

YOU WILL NEED:

◊ A can of shaving cream
◊ A rimmed baking sheet
◊ Spatula
◊ Food coloring
◊ A toothpick, butter knife, or pen for swirling

◊ Watercolor paper
◊ Paper towels
◊ A plastic ruler
◊ An adult to help

STEP 1: Spray shaving cream onto the baking sheet (make sure you ask an adult for permission first!), and smooth out the surface with a spatula. You'll want to use enough to create a bed that is larger than your paper and at least an inch thick. Set a couple of paper towels nearby as a place to put your finished paper.

STEP 2: Drop food coloring onto the surface of the shaving cream. Start by using one color and creating a polka-dot pattern. Use one or two drops of color in each spot. Then go back and add a second color in the white spaces between the first drops. Continue adding colors in the same way until you have a mix that you like. When you're done, you should have a multicolored polka-dot pattern.

STEP 3: Using a toothpick, swirl the colors together. Start by dragging the toothpick through one drop of color, then continue dragging until you get to another drop and drag through that. The toothpick should swirl color from the dots into the white cream around them. Without picking up the toothpick, continue connecting the dots until you've swirled through all of them and created a pattern that you like. Have fun playing with different directions and patterns!

STEP 4: Once you're happy with your pattern, carefully lay your paper on top of it and press down gently. The trick here is to make sure that the entire surface of your paper is touching the shaving cream, but avoid moving it from side to side, which can smear your design.

STEP 5: Leave the paper sitting on the shaving cream for at least 30 seconds, then carefully peel it up and lay it, shaving cream side up, on the paper towels. The pattern is supposed to look messy and blurred on this step, so don't worry.

STEP 6: With the paper lying flat on the table, use the edge of the ruler to scrape the shaving cream off in one smooth stroke. Your neat marble pattern will emerge on the paper beneath all that smeary shaving cream.

STEP 7: Use another paper towel to carefully blot any excess cream off the paper, then allow the design to air-dry.

Old chandelier crystals are a great way to light up a room with rainbows. You can find them in craft stores, thrift stores, or online. Thread a ribbon through the hole at the top of the crystal and hang it in a sunny window or in front of a desk lamp. When light shines through, the crystal acts as a prism, dividing the light into tiny rainbows that will appear around the room.

TIE-DYE IT

Way back in the '60s, people started tie-dying T-shirts. Back then, you could pretty much only use one color at a time, but now you can create a rainbow of colors. You can buy tie-dye kits or clothing dyes in craft stores or online. Just make sure that you protect work surfaces with a plastic sheet (working outdoors is an even better move) and follow any safety precautions on the dyes that you use. Here's how you can create a rainbow heart design on a T-shirt.

YOU'LL NEED:

◊ White cotton T-shirt
◊ Washable marker
◊ Rubber bands
◊ Latex gloves
◊ Fabric dye in squeeze bottles

STEP 1: Wash and dry your cotton shirt. Cover your work surface with plastic.

STEP 2: Lay the T-shirt on the protected work surface, and fold it in half lengthwise. Draw half of a heart along the fold using the washable marker.

STEP 3: Gather the fabric of the shirt along the line you have drawn. With one hand on each side of the line, start at the point and begin to scrunch the line together, creating an accordion fold. Keep scrunching around the shape of the heart, so that when you are done, the marker line has been compressed into one straight line. This gets tricky as you go around the curve of the heart—just do your best with each scrunch to touch the line on the new pleat to the line on the fabric you have already scrunched.

STEP 4: Once you've gathered the shirt together, tightly wrap a rubber band around the T-shirt so that it covers the line. Tie the rest of the shirt up with rubber bands every few inches or so.

STEP 5: Add color to the shirt. Wearing the latex gloves, start with the section between the end of the shirt and the line you drew. Saturate the fabric with dye from one of the squirt bottles. Be careful to go up to the rubber band but stay on one side of it, since that will define your heart shape.

STEP 6: Fill in the sections of fabric between the rest of the rubber bands with other colors of the rainbow. Flip the shirt over and color the other side of it to match the front side (make sure you use the same color on each section that you used on the first side).

STEP 7: Follow the directions on your dye package for setting the dye. This usually requires wrapping your shirt in plastic and letting it sit for several hours, then washing it.

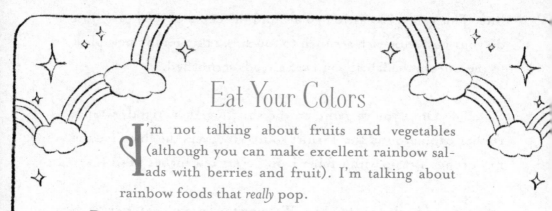

Eat Your Colors

I'm not talking about fruits and vegetables (although you can make excellent rainbow salads with berries and fruit). I'm talking about rainbow foods that *really* pop.

Rainbow ice cubes are as easy as, well, ice cubes. Fill an ice cube tray with water, add a couple of drops of food coloring to each cube, and swirl with a toothpick. Freeze the ice cubes as you normally would. When they're solid, fill up a glass with a rainbow of ice and cover with water, seltzer, or another see-through drink.

Jell-O parfait is an old-school treat that is as colorful as you can get. Use several packages of Jell-O in a rainbow of colors. Start by making one flavor, following the package directions, in the bottom of a glass bowl, casserole, or trifle dish. Cover the bowl with a plate or plastic wrap and put it in the refrigerator until the first layer has begun to set after about 2 hours. Mix up a different color, carefully pour it on top, then put it back in the fridge. Keep following the same process, adding each layer after the last has begun to set, until you've created as many layers as you'd like. You don't need to wait until each layer completely sets before you start the next one, but it needs to be firm enough that it is no longer a liquid, to prevent the layers from mixing. After you've poured the last layer, allow 4 hours for the entire parfait to set.

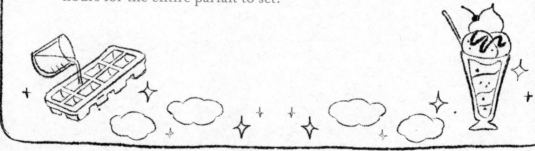

MAGIC MEADOW MUFFINS

If there's one thing unicorns and humans have in common, it's a love of sugar. These swirly, sparkly rainbow treats nod to your favorite mythical animal and are a great way to share your unicorn love with friends.

YOU'LL NEED:
◊ An adult to help
◊ The following ingredients

FOR THE CUPCAKES
◊ Cupcake tin and liners
◊ 1 box white cake mix, plus water, oil, and eggs as specified in the package instructions
◊ Food coloring (three different colors)

FOR THE FROSTING/ FILLING
◊ 1 stick butter, softened
◊ ¾ cup vegetable shortening
◊ 2¾ cup confectioner's sugar
◊ ½ teaspoon salt
◊ 1 teaspoon vanilla
◊ ½ teaspoon almond extract
◊ Sprinkles, decorator's sugar, or edible glitter

FOR DECORATION
◊ Shredded coconut and green food coloring
◊ Sprinkles, decorator's sugar, or edible glitter
◊ Marzipan (for bonus unicorn horn)

Preheat the oven. Line the cupcake tin with papers and set aside.

STEP 1: Make the cupcakes

Prepare the cake batter using the directions on the box.

Divide the batter into three smaller bowls, and add a different food coloring color to each. Red, yellow, and blue are good choices for a basic rainbow, but you can use any three colors. Go for pink, purple, and turquoise if that's more your style. If you are using regular food coloring, add a few drops to the bowl and stir to check color. If you are using gel colors, dip a toothpick into the color and then into the batter and stir. If it doesn't look bright enough, add more, a bit at a time, until you are happy with the color.

Fill the cupcake liners in layers: Pour until they are about one third full with one color of batter. Slowly pour the second color of batter on top of it until the liner is about two thirds full. Pour the third color on top of that, stopping short of the top of the liner so that the batter won't overflow as it rises. (Don't worry if your layers don't stay perfect. They're going to swirl together anyway.)

You can use a toothpick to gently swirl the colors together (See? Told you so.) or leave them to create surprise color patterns as they bake.

Bake according to the package directions.

STEP 2: Make the frosting

Cream together butter and shortening. Add sugar, salt, vanilla, and almond extract, and beat until the ingredients are completely combined and the frosting has a light, airy consistency.

Scoop about one third of the finished frosting into a smaller bowl.

Add decorator's sugar, sprinkles, or edible glitter to the frosting in the small bowl and stir it in. Add as much or as little as you want. These are *your* cupcakes!

With the mixer running, drop green food coloring into the main bowl of frosting until it reaches a bright, grassy green.

STEP 3: Make the grass

Drop shredded coconut into a Ziploc bag with green food coloring. Rub the coconut and coloring together until the coconut turns green.

STEP 4: Assemble the cupcakes

Using an apple corer, cut a hole down from the top of the cupcake right through the middle. If you don't have an apple corer, you can use a knife, a spoon, or a small melon baller to scoop it out. Try not to break through the bottom of the cupcake.

Fill the cupcakes with the sparkly frosting from the small bowl. (You may want to drop some sprinkles, red hots, or other small candy into the bottom of the hole first—this is a great place to be creative and hide edible surprises.)

Frost the cupcakes with green frosting, and sprinkle the shredded coconut over the top. Create a ring of flower sprinkles or miniature flowers around the outside of the cupcake "meadow."

BONUS STEP: Add a horn

If you want to make your cupcakes extra unicorny, break out the marzipan. Marzipan is a paste made of almonds and sugar that you can mold and model a little like Play-Doh. (Not exactly like Play-Doh—you need to treat it gently.)

To make a unicorn horn, take a piece of marzipan about the size of a large marble and split it into two pieces. Roll each between your palm and a clean surface to create an elongated cone shape. Put the two cones side by side and gently twist them together. (You will only get a twist or two before the marzipan breaks.) Roll the twisted horn under your palm to smooth out the twist and bring the horn back to shape. Pinch the point to make sure it's sharp.

Bibliography

HISTORY

The following books and websites were used as reference on unicorn history and lore. They are excellent resources for anyone interested in learning more about the subject.

BOOKS

Freeman, Margaret B. *The Unicorn Tapestries*. New York: Metropolitan Museum of Art, 1976.

Giblin, James Cross, illustrated by Michael McDermott. *The Truth About Unicorns*. New York: HarperCollinsPublishers, 1991.

Giblin, James Cross, illustrated by Claire Ewart. *The Dwarf, the Giant, and the Unicorn: A Tale of King Arthur*. New York: Clarion Books, 1995.

Laskow, Sarah, illustrated by Sam Beck. *The Very Short, Entirely True History of Unicorns.* New York: Penguin Workshop, 2019.

Pilling, Ann, illustrated by Kady MacDonald Denton. *The Kingfisher Treasury of Myths and Legends.* London: Kingfisher, 2003.

Shepard, Odell. *The Lore of the Unicorn.* New York: Crown Publishers, 1982.

WEBSITES

The Editors of Encyclopaedia Britannica, "Unicorns: They Exist." Encyclopaedia Britannica, Inc. August 31, 2018. https://www.britannica.com/topic/Unicorns-They-Exist-2130405#ref1259909, accessed November 2019.

"Mythic Creatures." Chicago: The Chicago Field Museum. archive.fieldmuseum.org/mythiccreatures/index.html, accessed December 2019.

"Mythic Creatures." New York: The American Museum of Natural History. www.amnh.org/exhibitions/mythic-creatures, accessed December 2019.

"The Unicorn: Museum Stories Pamphlets Numbers 227–235." Chicago: The Chicago Natural History Museum, 1952. https://archive.org/details/museumstoriespa58/page/2, accessed December 2019.

POPCORN

You can read all the books and watch all the shows listed in the PopCorn section. They're out there waiting for you to check them out.

NOVELS

Beagle, Peter S. *The Last Unicorn.* New York: Penguin Books, 1968.

Carroll, Lewis. *Through the Looking Glass.* London: Macmillan (1871).

Cavallaro, Mike. *Nico Bravo and the Hound of Hades.* New York: First Second, 2019.

Coville, Bruce. *Into the Land of the Unicorns.* New York: Scholastic, 1994.

Goudge, Elizabeth. *The Little White Horse.* London: University of London Press, 1946.

L'Engle, Madeleine. *A Swiftly Tilting Planet.* New York: Farrar, Strauss, and Giroux, 1978.

Lewis, C. S. *The Last Battle.* London: The Bodley Head, 1956.

Ogburn, Janet, illustrated by Rebecca Green. *The Unicorn in the Barn.* Boston: HMH Books for Young Readers, 2017.

Simpson, Dana. *Phoebe and Her Unicorn.* Kansas City: Andrews McMeel Publishing, 2016.

Yolen, Jane. *The Transfigured Hart.* New York: Harcourt, 1975.

FILMS

The Fantastic Adventures of Unico. Directed by Toshio Hirata and Osamu Tezuka, Sanrio Communications, 1981.

Harry Potter and the Sorcerer's Stone. Directed by Chris Columbus, Warner Bros., 2001.

The Last Unicorn. Directed by Jules Bass and Arthur Rankin, Jr. Rankin/Bass Productions, 1982.

Legend. Directed by Ridley Scott, Legend Production, 1985.

The Lego Movie. Directed by Christopher Miller and Phil Lord, Warner Bros., 2015.

The Lion, the Witch and the Wardrobe. Directed by Andrew Adamson, Walt Disney Pictures, 2007.

My Little Pony: The Movie. Directed by Jason Thiessen, Lionsgate, 2017.

Nico the Unicorn. Directed by Graeme Campbell, American Cinema Productions, 1998.

The Secret of Moonacre. Directed by Gabor Csupo, Forgan-Smith Entertainment, 2008.

Stardust. Directed by Matthew Vaughn, Paramount Pictures, 2007.

Toy Story 3. Directed by Lee Unkrich, Walt Disney Pictures/Pixar Animation Studio, 2010.

Unicorn Store. Directed by Brie Larson, produced by 51 Entertainment, 2019.

TV SHOWS

She-Ra: Princess of Power. Produced by Filmation Associates and Mattel, three seasons, 1985–87.

She-Ra and the Princesses of Power. Produced by DreamWorks Animation Television and Mattel, first season 2018.

My Little Pony: Friendship Is Magic. Allspark Animation, first season 2010.

UNICORNS TODAY

The information included in the Unicorns Today section came entirely from the mind of the author and isn't necessarily accurate, precise, or even true.

Index

About the Creators

PENELOPE GWYNNE believes that the secret to finding unicorns in the wild is to first get in touch with the unicorn within. A leading expert in unicorn husbandry and tracking, she also works as a children's book editor and writer. When she's not traveling the world in search of magical beasts, she makes her home in New York's Hudson River Valley.

KATIE O'NEILL is a self-taught writer and illustrator based in New Zealand. She's interested in nature and all kinds of creatures, mindfulness, and finding joy in everyday life. Her graphic novels for children have won Eisner, Harvey, and Dwayne McDuffie Awards, and have been featured on the ALA Rainbow List.

Thank you for reading this Feiwel & Friends book.

The friends who made

For Unicorn Lovers Only
History, Mythology, Facts, and More

possible are:

JEAN FEIWEL, Publisher

LIZ SZABLA, Associate Publisher

RICH DEAS, Senior Creative Director

HOLLY WEST, Senior Editor

ANNA ROBERTO, Senior Editor

KAT BRZOZOWSKI, Senior Editor

DAWN RYAN, Senior Managing Editor

KIM WAYMER, Senior Production Manager

EMILY SETTLE, Associate Editor

ERIN SIU, Associate Editor

RACHEL DIEBEL, Assistant Editor

FOYINSI ADEGBONMIRE, Editorial Assistant

LIZ DRESNER, Associate Art Director

PERRY MINELLA, Assistant Managing Editor

Follow us on Facebook or visit us online at mackids.com.
Our books are friends for life.